COMPUTER OPERATOR & PROGRAMMING ASSISTANT

COMPUTER OPERATOR & PROGRAMMING ASSISTANT

MANOJ DOLE

Digitization is the need of the time. In the future, training in industrial training institutes will need to be conducted using online internet to make training more convenient and easy. E-books containing a set of MCQ questions will be made available to the trainees as they need to be more accustomed to the multiple choice questions MCQ to prepare for the online exams taking place in their industrial training institutes.

With all these factors in mind, Mr. Manoj Madhukar Dole Instructor, Industrial Training Institute, Satara, has written books according to the new annual system and NSQF-5 syllabus. And they've created theoretical mobile apps and blogs to make training easier, and made all these educational materials available for download on the world famous websites Google Play Store, Amazon and Apple Book Store.

The books were published by Hon'ble Joint Director Shri Rajendra Ghume Saheb Regional Office of Vocational Education and Training, Pune on 9/1/2019, at this time Shri Prakash Saigavkar Saheb Principal Government Industrial Training Institute Aundh Pune, Shri Tukaram Misal Saheb Principal Govt. Q. Sanstha Satara, Shri Sachin Dhumal Saheb District Vocational Education and Training Officer Satara, Shri Yatin Pargaonkar Saheb Principal Govt. Q. Sanstha Kolhapur, Shri Vikas Teke Saheb Inspector Vocational Education and Training Regional Office Pune, Palekar Foods Products Pvt. Ltd. Entrepreneurial Chairman of Satara Mr. Nilkanthrao Palekar Saheb, Chairman of Hira Foods Mr. Ibrahim Baba Tamboli Saheb, Mrs. Shalmali Pawar Headmaster Government Technical School Center Satara and other dignitaries were present on the occasion.

Contents

Prologue

Computer Operator & Programming Assistant is a simple e-Book for ITI & Engineering Course Computer Operator & Programming Assistant, Revised NSQF Syllabus, It contains objective questions with underlined & bold correct answers MCQ covering all topics including all about the latest & Important about about safety and environment, use of fire extinguishers. trade tools, identifies computer peripherals, internal components, basic DOS commands, Windows and Linux interface and its related software installation. MS Office word document, excel sheet and power point presentation, database with MS Access. network system of an organization. internet browser basic static webpage using HTML. JavaScript and dynamic webpage and hosting technique in a registered domain. VBA to create & edit various types of macros in MS Excel and to develop user form using VBA. accounting software Tally. E-commerce system and E-commerce websites. cyber crimes secure information from Internet by cyber security concept.

Foreword

Vocational education and training is imparted through the Department of Vocational Education and Training through the Department of Business Education and Business Practical to supply multi-skilled artisans in line with the rapidly growing demand in the industrial sector in the 21st century. All the occupations within the institutions are important, as the trainees from these occupations develop multi-skills as per the demands of the industry.

with the noble intention of making available MCQ e-books suitable for all businesses, considering that all the examinations in all the industries in the industrial sector are conducted online and include MCQ method questions. Mr. Manoj Madhukar Dole has written a very good e-book on MCQ method as per the new annual syllabus. This e-book will definitely be a guide for all the trainees, trainee candidates, training instructors and others concerned.

The author of the book is Mr. Manoj Madhukar Dole, Instructor Gov. ITI Satara has 17 years of training experience. Written as a new annual pattern, this e-book incorporates modern digital QR Code technology to understand the layout, simple language, and simple syntax, diagrams and videos for each subject. So I am sure that this e-book will definitely be useful for in-depth study and exam practice. The work they have done is certainly commendable.

Mr. Tukaram Misal
Principal Government Industrial Training Institute Satara.

Preface

DGET New Delhi and CSTARI Kolkata have been implementing an annual pattern for all businesses in ITI since the August 2018 session. The examination system will also be changed and it will be online from this year and since all the questions are of Objective Type (MCQ), the trainees are in dire need of in-depth study. It is with this in mind that we are delighted to present the books based on the old NIMI pattern and a complete overview of the new annual pattern, and we hope that these books will be a guide for all business directors and trainees. Is.

For writing these books, Johar Awate Saheb, Principal of ITI Akluj. Former Principal of ITI Satara Saigavkar Saheb, Assistant Director Shri Chandrakant Dhekne Saheb Regional Office of Vocational Education and Training, Pune, District Vocational Education and Training Officer Sachin Dhumal Saheb and Headmaster Government Technical School Kendra Shalmali Pawar Madam and son Adhiraj Dole, mother Kusum Dole, I am very grateful to my father Madhukar Dole and wife Ashwini Dole for their special guidance and cooperation from time to time.

Also, in a very short period of time, the book was reviewed by Shri Rajendra Ghume Saheb, Joint Director, Vocational Education and Training Regional Office, Pune, for his invaluable time in publishing the book. I am sincerely grateful for their feedback.

I am grateful to the Instructor of ITI Satara for there continuous support from the very beginning of writing the book.

From this book, I consider myself blessed to have shared my thoughts on e-learning with you. I will not claim that this book is perfect, because considering the perfection, this book is an attempt and is in its infancy. They will be valuable for improvement if they are tested and suggested.

Manoj Dole
Dated 9/1/2019

Acknowledgements

The industrial training and theoretical examination system of our industrial training institutes and these changes have been accepted by the craft instructors and the trainees. Theoretical examinations conducted in your industrial training institutes are also conducted online. Since these examinations are of multiple choice MCQ method, the trainees will need to get more practice of such questions.

With all these considerations in mind, Mr. Manoj Madhukar, Director, Dole Crafts, Katari Industrial Training Institute, Satara, has done a thorough study and with his diligent work and added his keen intellect, according to the new annual system and NSQF-5 syllabus, e-book of Katari and other machine trades. -Book) and they have created mobile apps and blogs on theoretical topics to make training easier and have made all these educational materials available for download on the world famous websites Google Play Store, Amazon and Apple Book Store. Training has been made easier by creating a print version and using advanced techniques like QR Code.

All these educational materials will definitely be a guide for all the trainees for in-depth study and for the craft instructors and other concerned who are imparting vocational training.

CHAPTER ONE

Computer Operator & Programming Assistant MCQ Drawings

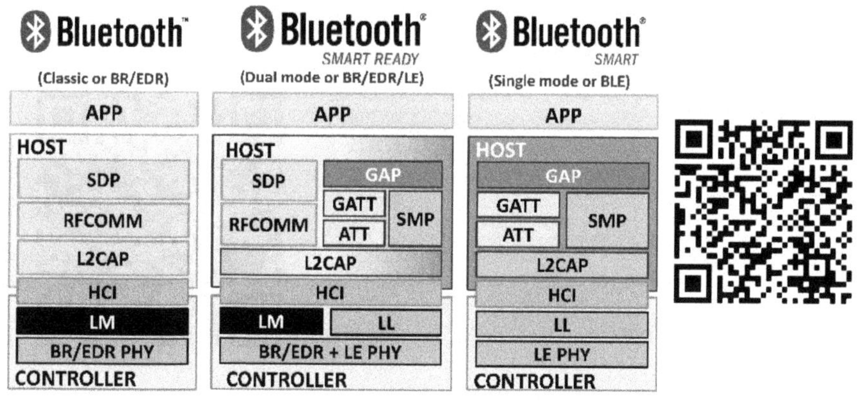

Bluetooth Configuration

What is a Browser - Definition and Types

Browser-Definition-and-Types

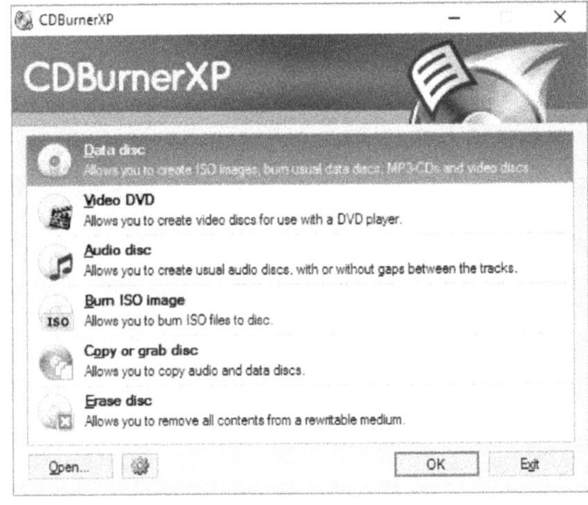

CDBurnerXP

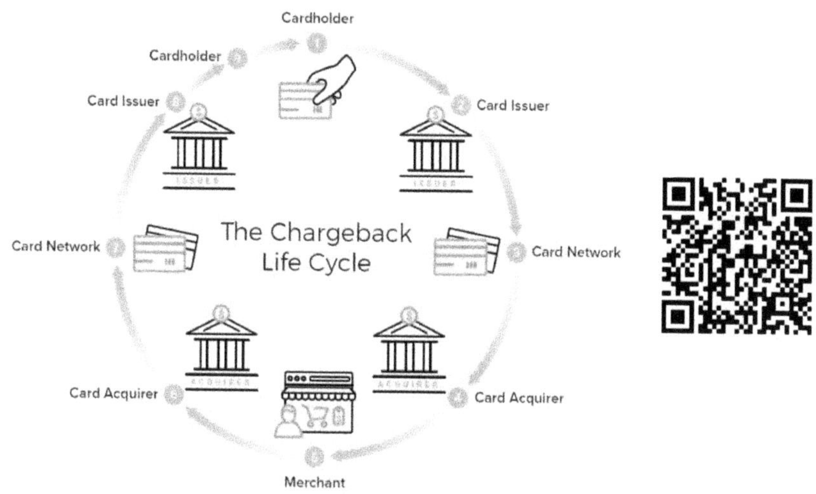

Chargeback system

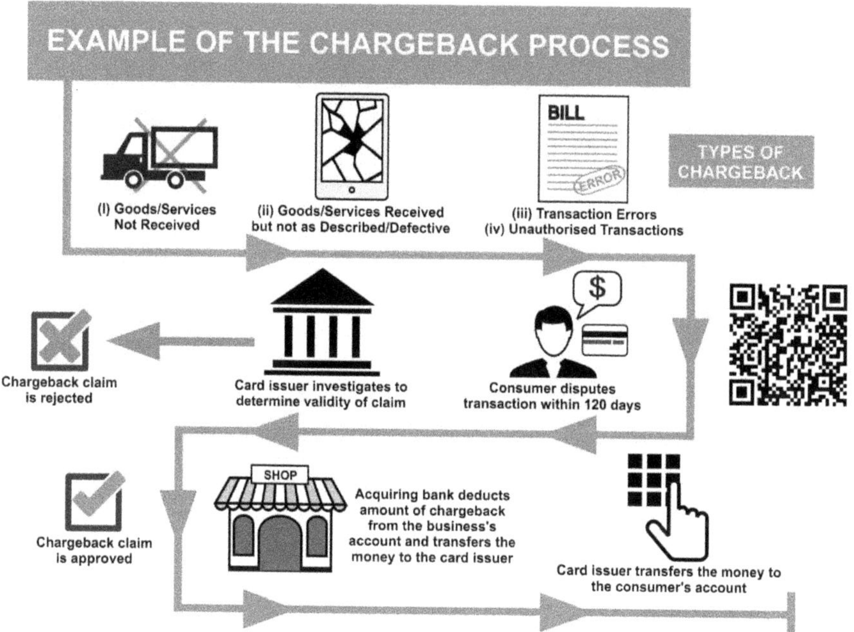

Chargeback system 2

css & html website

Cyber Security

Domain-Name-System

Domain-Name-System

Domain-Name-System

Domain-Name-System 2

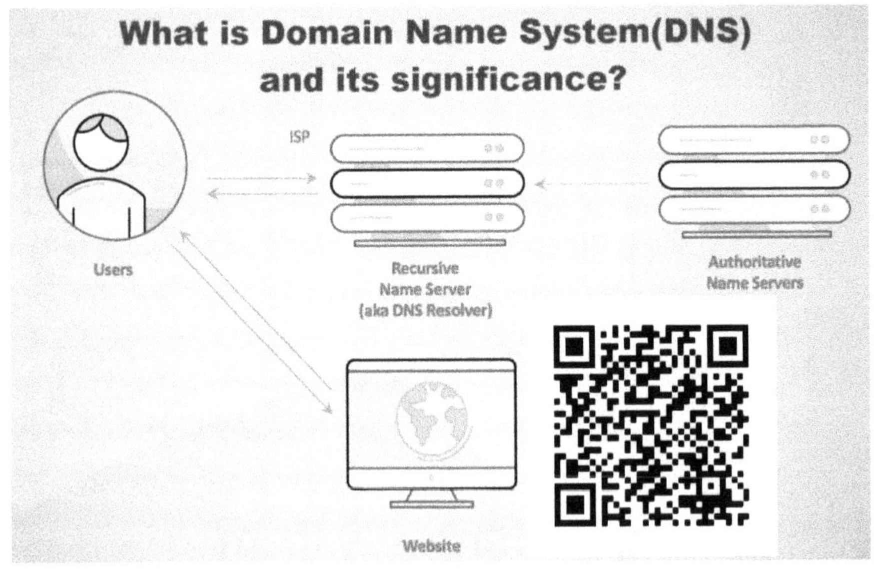

Domain-Name-System 3

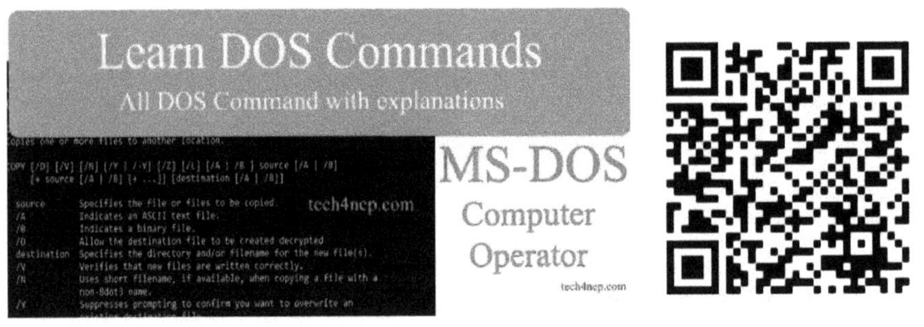

DOS-Command

Driver Installation & Update

ecommerce 2

THE 8 BENEFITS OF HAVING AN E-COMMERCE
WEBSITE IN TODAY'S BUSINESS SCENARIO
Sell Quickly
Low Cost
Shoppers begin the hunt Online
Insight on Customer Data
Reach Out To New Customers
Strategy for Content Marketing
Serving the Niche Markets
Meet Customers at their location

ecommerce 3

Business to business

Business to consumer

Consumer to consumer

Consumer to business

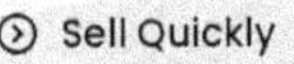

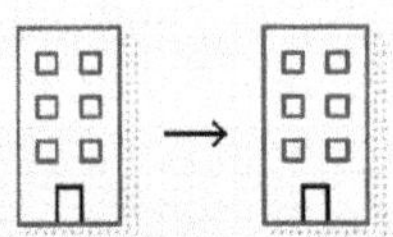

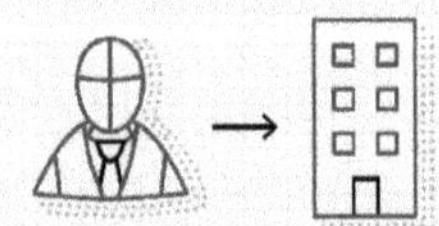

ecommerce types 1

ecommerce types

Email

HTML web design

internet online business

internet-business-models

JavaScript

linux-operating-system

MICROSOFT-ACCESS

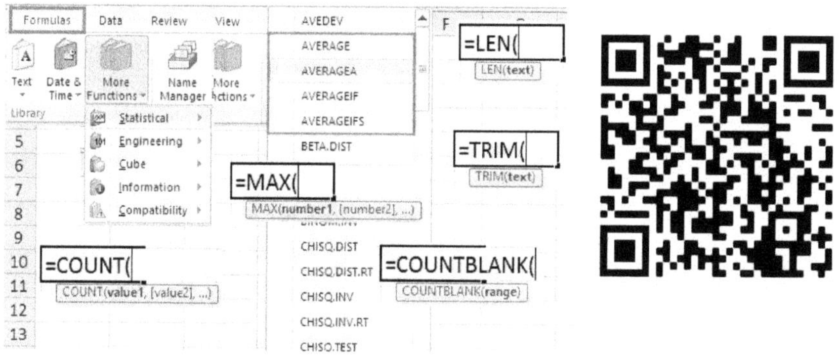

MS Excel-Basic-Functions

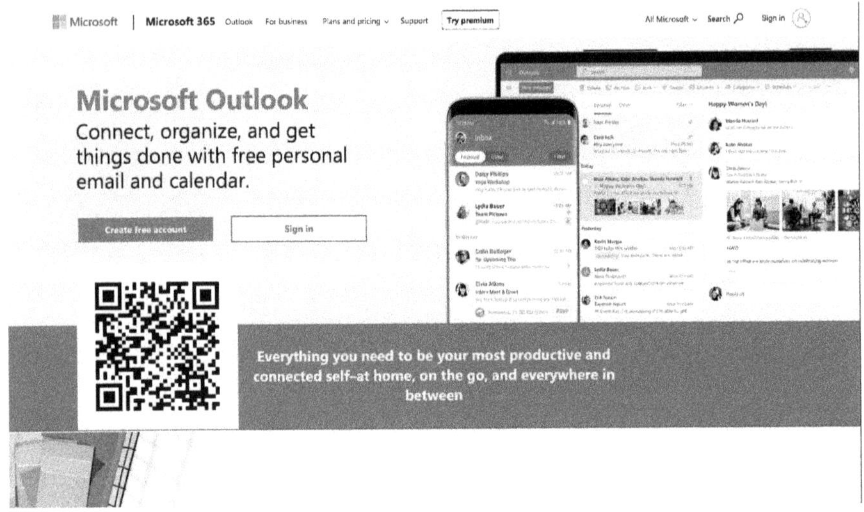

ms outlook

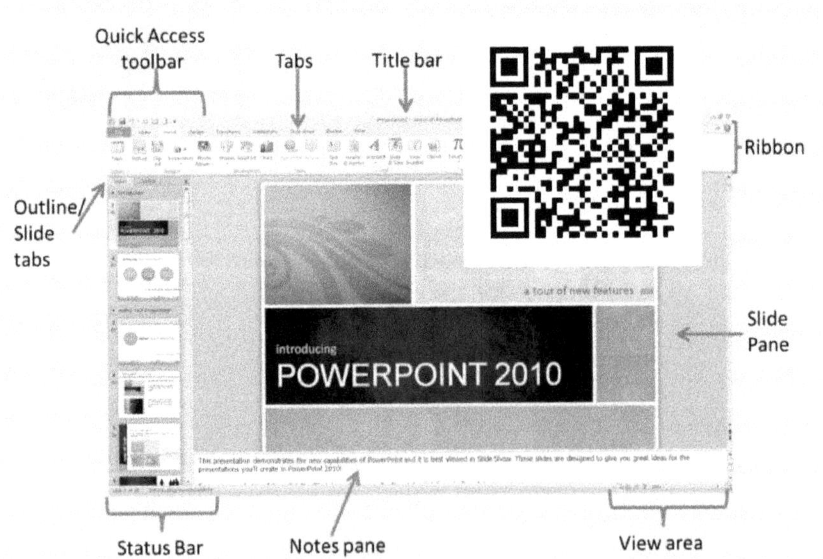

ms power-point

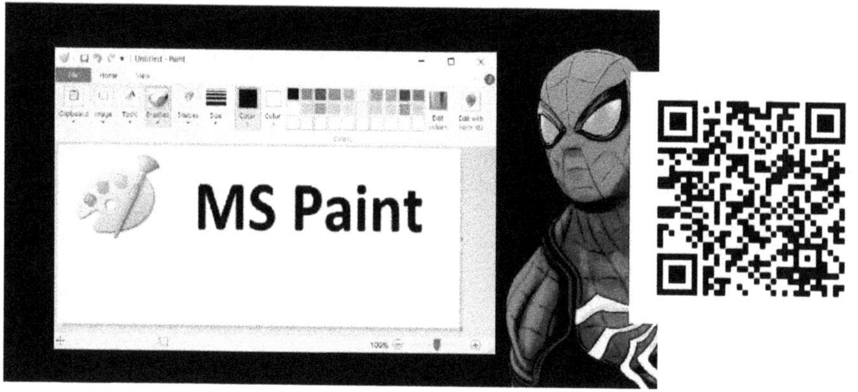

ms-paint

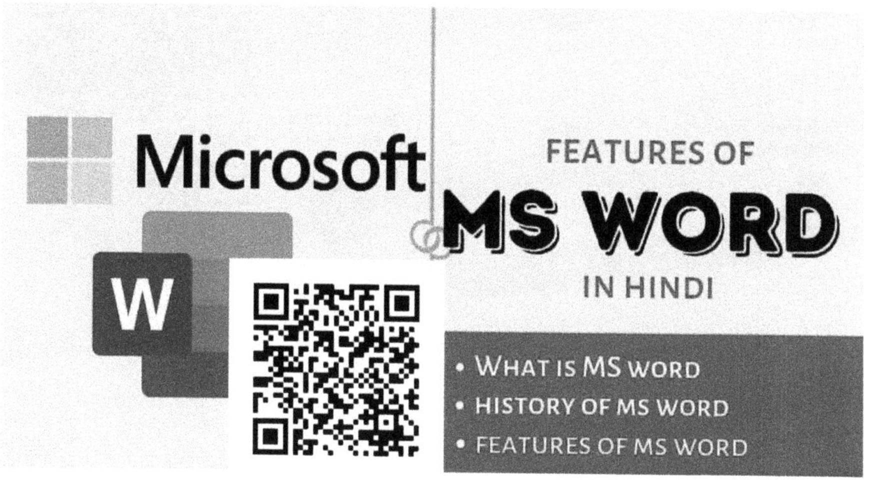

ms-word

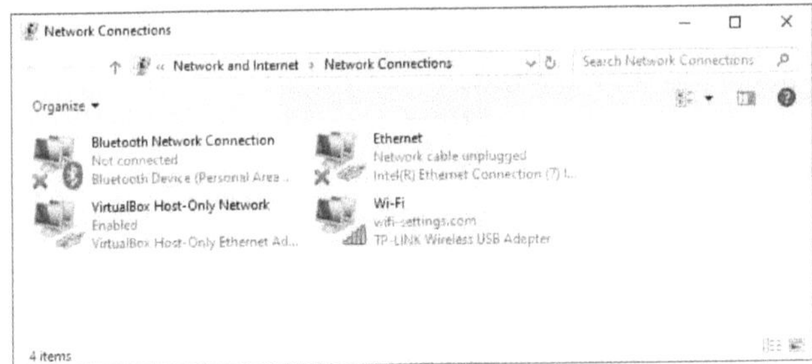

Network-Connections

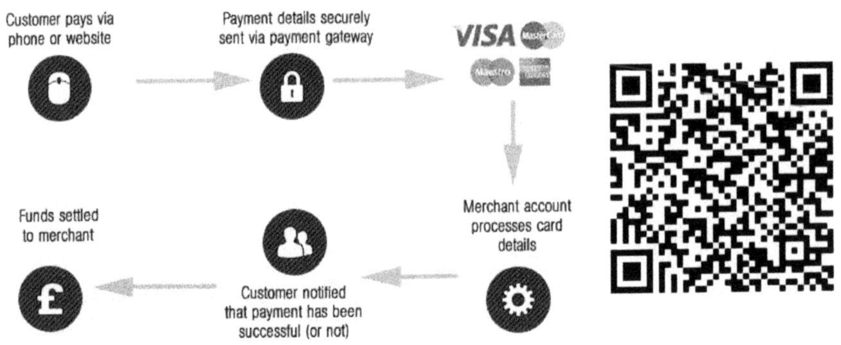

Payment and Order Processing 1

Payment and Order Processing 3

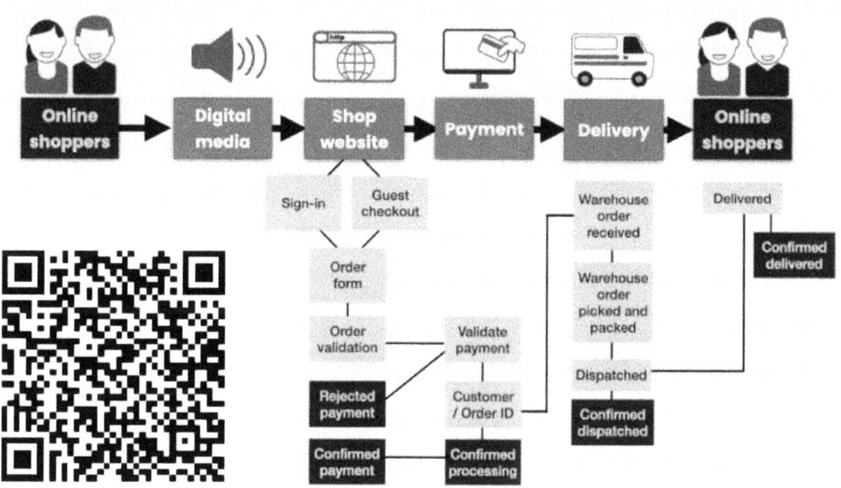

Payment and Order Processing 4

Payment and Order Processing

Payment-Gateways

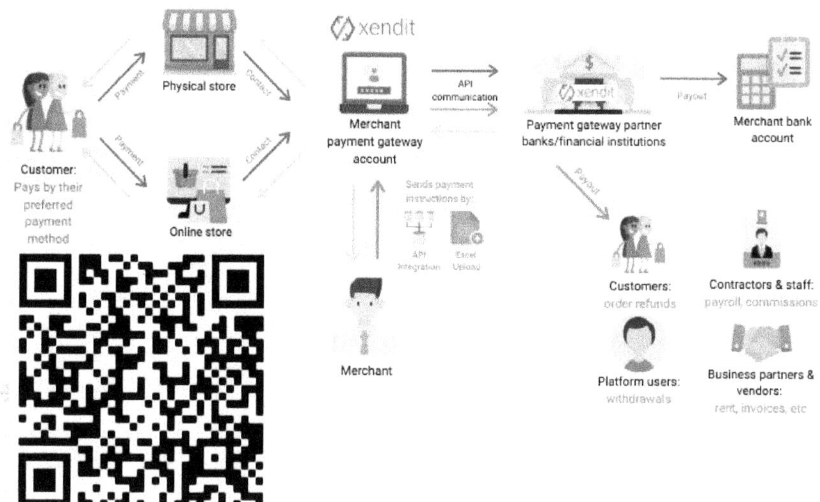

payment-gateways-work

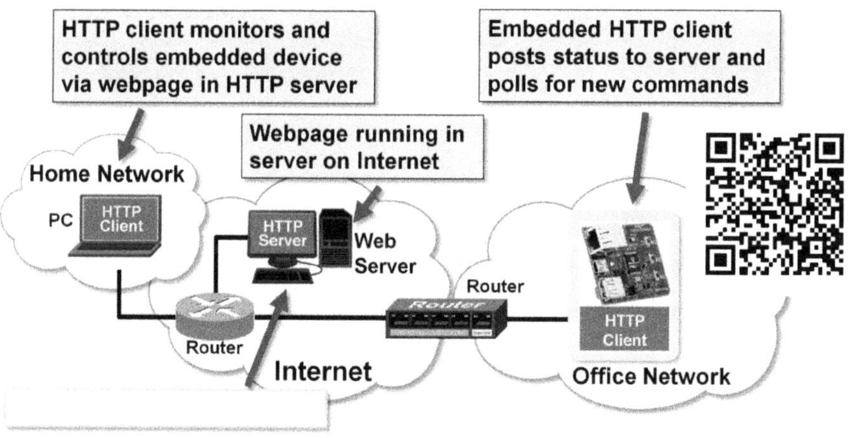

server 1

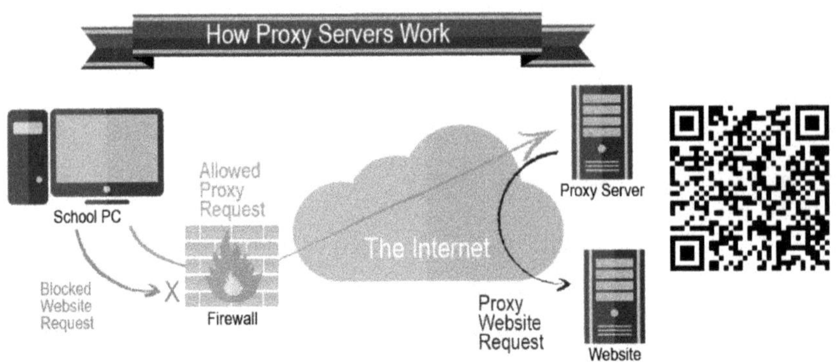

server

Social-Networking-Sites

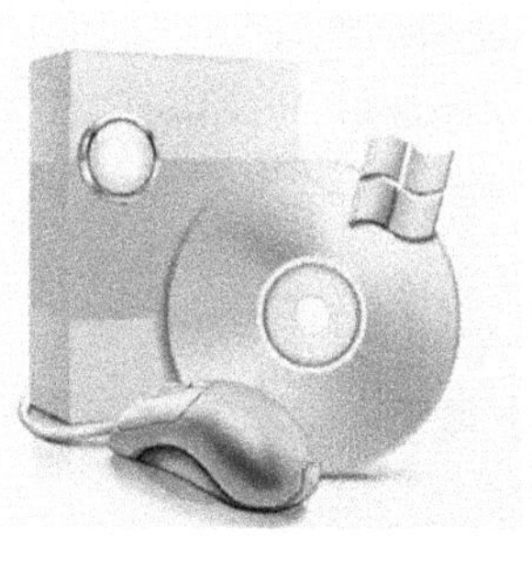

software-installation

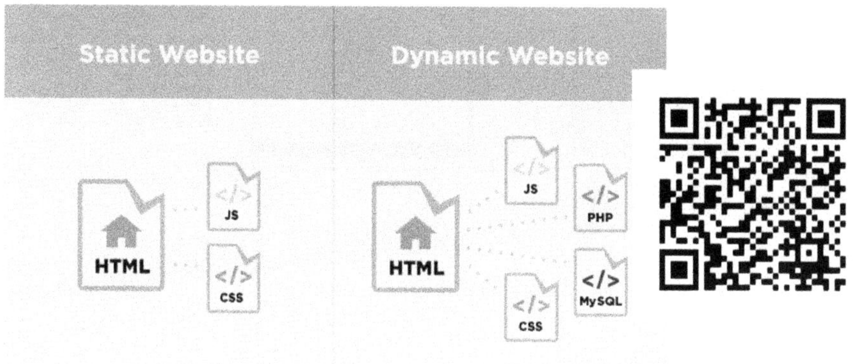

static dynamic web page 1

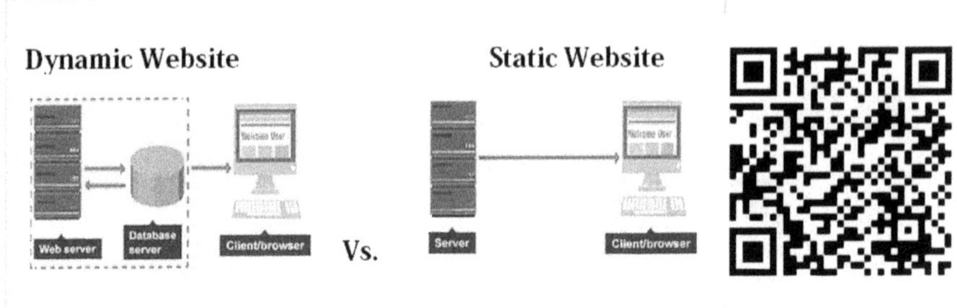

static dynamic web page

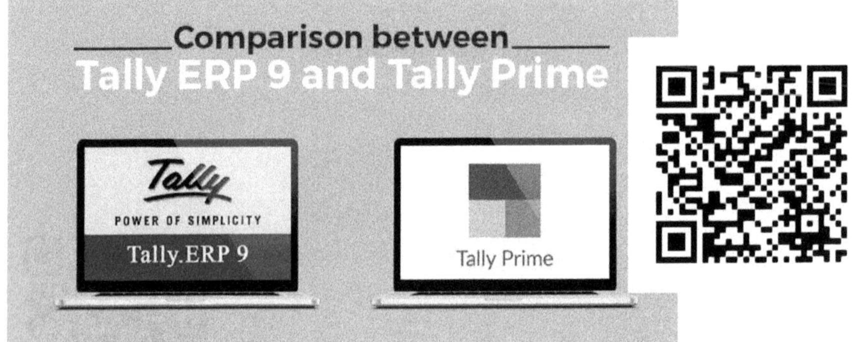

Tally.ERP-9-and-TallyPrime

uses-of-internet

vba-excel-language

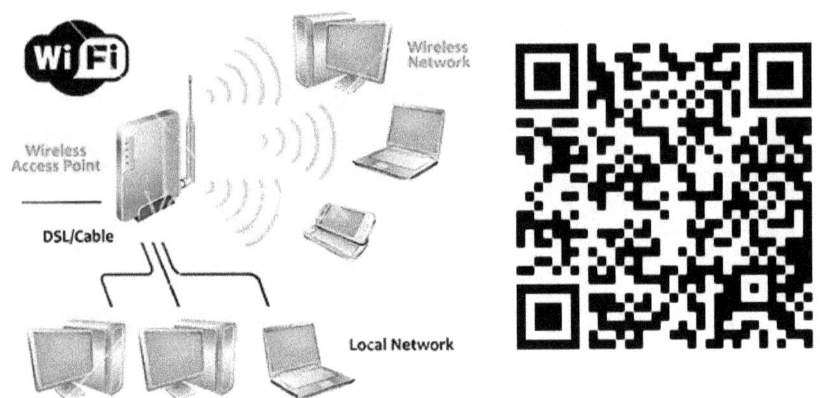

wifi-networks

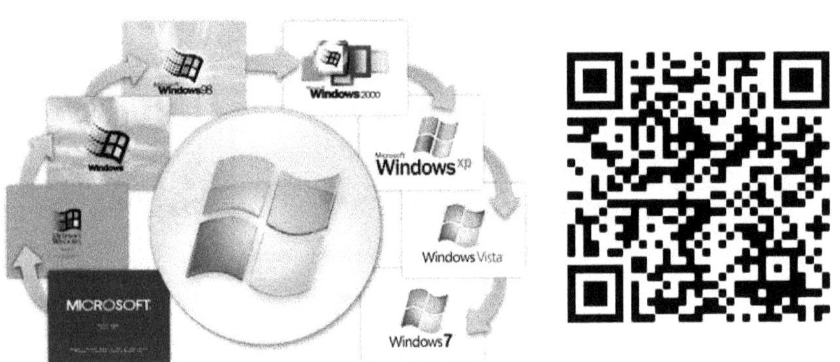

windows-operating-system

WWW

CHAPTER TWO

Computer Operator & Programming Assistant MCQ

1] ABC stands for --------------

A] Automatic Breathing Control

B] Automatic Blood Control

C] Airway Breathing Circulation

D] Automatic Blood Circulation

3] To put off"Class B" fire, the types of fire extinguisher used is ....

A] dry power

B] Carbon dioxide

C] Jet of water

D] Foam type

4] Which type of fire extinguisher is used to put off general fire?

A] Water type Extinguisher

B] Foam type Extinguisher

C] Dry chemical powder Extinguisher

D] Carbon dioxide (C02] Extinguisher

5] In case of bleeding, take treatment Of

D] cold 3" and rest

A] spray cold water

B] Bandage immediately -----.

B] Enquire about the accident thought treatment

6] in case of an accident, the victim should im

A] Asked to take rest

C] Attended immediately

D] leave him

7] First aid is given to an injured or ill person primarily....

A] Save life

B] Prevent further deterioration of the muff's

C] Give best possible comfort

D] All of these

Q.1. Which of the following is the biggest unit of memory?

A] Gigabytes.

B] bytes.

C] Megabytes.

D] Kilobytes.

Q.2. The primary purpose of software is to turn data into.

A] Website.

B] Infromation.

C] Programs.

D] Objects.

Q.3. GUI Stands for

A] Graphical User Interface.

B] Greater User Interface.

C] Graphical Union Interface.

D] Graphical User Intereat.

Q.4. Key board keys that have arrows on them are called -

A] Function Keys.

B] Navigation Keys.

C] Typewriter Keys.

D] Special purpose keys.

Q.5. ASSCII, EBCDIC and Unicode are examples of Application Software's

A] True.

B] False.

Q.6. The easiest way to access any part of the screen in the windows operating system is using the.

A] Key Board.

B] Rat.

C] Mouse.

D]] Joystick.

Q.7. A software is also called as a

A] Procedure.

B] Data.

C] Programs.

D] Information.

Q.8. Back programs make copies of the files to be used in case the original files are damaged or lost.

A] True.

B] False.

Q.9. Microprocessor is often called as CPU

A] True.

B] False.

Q.10. .... Utility identifies unnecessary files on the hard disk and erases them based on users command.

A] Backup.

B] File Compression.

C] Uninstall Programs.

D]] Disk Clean up.

Q.11. This type of software is designs to help you be more productive tasks, and is widely used in nearly every disc live and occupation.

A] Communication Software.

B] Utility Software.

C] Basic Application Software.

D] System Software.

Q.12. Minicomputers are also known as.

A] Mid Range Computers.

B] Personal Digital Computers.

C] Mainframe Computers.

D] Laptop Computers.

Q.13. Which of the following device is used to play fast games on a computers.

A] Touch Surface.

B] Touch Screen.2

C] Track Ball.

D] Joystick.

Q.14. Which of the following would not be considered as portable computer.

A] Desktop Computer.

B] Note book computer.

C] Personal Digital Assistant.

D] None of these.

Q.15. Headphone is a typical output device.

A] True.

B] False.

Q.16. Uninstall programs help us to remove unwanted programs installed in the computer.

A] True.

B] False.

Q.17. The capacity of a storage device is usually measured in terms of bytes.

A] True.

B] False.

Q.18. Capacity of the storage device is usually measured in terms of meter.

A] True.

B] False.

Q.19............. is a pointing device.

A] Mouse.

B] Printer.

C] Scanner.

D] Keyboard.

Q.20. The keyboards keys that are labelled F1, F2 and so on are called ....

A] Function Keys.

B] Numeric Keys.

C] Typewriter Keys.

D] Special purpose keys.

Q.21. The keyboard keys like Caps lock that turn on features on or off are called.

A] Function Keys.

B] Combination Keys.

C] Toggle Keys.

D] Special Purpose Keys.

Q.22. Word processing, electronic spread sheets, database managers and graphics programs are all grouped under the title.

A] Browsings Programs.

B] Operating System.

C] Application Software.

D] Data and Information.

Q.23. Keyboard, mouse, monitor, and system unit collectively also known as

A] Solid ware.

B] Software.

C] Hardware.

D] Firm ware.

Q.24. Output of an image on the monitor screen is often called soft copy.

A] True.

B] False.

Q.25. each 0 and 1 in the binary numbering system is called a bit.

A] True.

B] False.

Q.26. Catch memory is used to store most frequently accessed information from the RAM.

A] True.

B] False.

Q.27. The system board is also known as the main board or mother board.

A] True.

B] False.

Q.28. ASSCII, EBCDIC and Unicode are binary coding schemes.

A] True.

B] False.

Q.29. The keys labelled 0-9 on the keyboard are called.

A] Function Keys.

B] Numeric Keys.

C] Typewriter Keys.

D] Special purpose keys.

Q.30. A CD ROM stands for Compact Disk Read Only Memory.

A] True.

B] False.

Q.31. .... consists of step-by-step introductions that tells the computer how to complete the task.

A] Programs.

B] Hardware.

C] Data.

D] Objects.

Q.32. A CD-R stands for CD-Recordable.

A] True.

B] False.

Q.33.......... is a background soft ware that helps the computer to manage its internal resources.

A] System Software.

B] Information.

C] Objects.

D] None of these.

Q.34. Output of an image obtained using a printer is called as hard copy.

A] True.

B] False.

Q.35. Following are the file compression programs, EXCEPT

A] Win Zip.

B] RAID.

C] Win RAR.

D] PK Zip.

Q.36. A track on a disk is one of the many circular ring areas where data is written magnetically.

A] True.

B] False.

Q.37. Floppy disks are removable storage media.

A] True.

B] False.

Q.38. The keyboard keys that have arrows on them are called.

A] Function Keys.

B] Combination Keys.

C] Navigation Keys

D] Special Purpose Keys.

Q.39. Microprocessor is often called as CPU.

A] True.

B] False.

Q.40. Eight bits make up a bite.

A] True.

B] False.

Q.41. Output of an image on the monitor screen is often called hard copy.

A] True.

B] False.

Q.42.......... are graphical objects used to represent and open commonly used applications.

A] G.U.I..

B] Primers'.

C] Windows NT.

D] Icons.

Q.43. A CD-ROM means CD-RW.

A] True.

B] False.

Q.44. Data stored in RAM is

A] Is non-volatile.

B] Is only there while the power is on.

C] Remains only a few minutes after the power is turned off.

D] Is permanent and only lost in power failure.

Q.45. A CD-R stands for CD-Regional.

A] True.

B] False.

Q.46. Primary function of a monitor is to display information to the user.

A] True.

B] False.

Q.47. Random Access Memory] RAM. is .... type of memory.

A] Permanent.

B] Temporary.

C] Flash.

D] Smart.

Q.48 The external memory of the computer is present on the motherboard in the form of slots.

A] False.

B] True.

Q.49 The internal memory of the computer is present on the motherboard in the form of chips

A] True.

B] False.

Q.50 cache memory is used to store most frequently accessed information from the ram.

A] True.

B] False.

Q.1. The "System Date" and "System Time" are the date and time as maintained by the computer's internal clock.

A] True

B] False

Q.2. Disk cleanup is used to rearrange your files so that they are not broken up.

A] True

B] False

Q.3. In Window Vista a folder system is also called a "Directory System."

A] True

B] False

Q.4. "rtf" stands for "rich text format"

A] True

B] False

Q.5. You can click on.............. to learn how to use Windows Vista, obtain troubleshooting information, receive support and more.

A] "Search"

B] "Windows"

C] "Start"

D] "Help & Support"

Q.6. In MS paint to draw a curved line, we have to click the.................... Icon.

A] "Curve"

B] "Line"

C] "Polygon"

D] "Rectangle"

Q.7. .... refers to the height and width of the characters to be printed.

A] "Font Size"

B] "Border"

C] "Cell"

D] "Font Style"

Q.8. There is button which is not present on the "Title bar".

A] Minimize

B] Start

C] Maximise

D] Close

Q.9. Disk Defragmenter is used to remove unnecessary files on your hard disk to free up space and your computer run faster.

A] True

B] False

Q.10. To change the size of your picture, Select "Image Attributes" from the menu.

A] True

B] False

Q.11. To start the calculator application click "Start" and select "All Programs Accessories Calculator."

A] True

B] False

Q.12. .... can be used to create and format large and complex text documents.

A] "Calculator"

B] "WordPad"

C] "Notepad"

D] "Text Pad"

Q.13. Notepad is a basic text editor that can be used to create simple documents.

A] True

B] False

Q.14. A folder system is also called a "................"

A] "Direction System"

B] "Directory System"

C] "Directory list"

D] "Folder book"

Q.15. A folder within a folder is known as a "Folder list."

A] True

B] False

Q.17. A .... is like a container in which you can store files.

A] "Icon"

B] "document"

C] "Folder"

D] "Sheet"

Q.18. The operating system's job is .... to

A] Execute many useful commands easily.

B] to make request for service through a defined application programme interface.

C] to control the computer at the most fundamental level.

D] None of these.

Q.19. The windows interface is based on ....

A] "Graphical user Interface" or GUI

B] Application Programme Interface or] API.

C] "Clipboard"

D] None of these

Q.20. The name of a file consists of two parts, the File Name and the sub file name.

A] True

B] False

Q.21. To access the location of the particular file quickly, you create a shortcut icon for the file and place it on the desktop.

A] True

B] False

Q.22. In Windows Vista windows sidebar contains mini-programs called gadgets.

A] True

B] False

Q.23. A file created using Notepad is stored with the extension.................. .

A] ".txt"

B] ".docx"

C] ".png"

D] ".jpg"

Q.24. In windows vista two types of "searchers" are supported: Regular search Instant search.

A] True

B] False

Q.25. When your computer is booted and is ready to use, the screen you see is called the ....

A] "Table top"

B] "Desktop"

C] "Laptop"

D] None of these

Q.26. "Computer" is an application which performs functions same as that of a handheld calculator.

A] True

B] False

Q.27. .... is designed to prevent and remove spy ware.

A] User Account Control

B] Windows Firewall

C] Windows Defender

D] Parental Controls

Q.28. The clipboard is not available in Windows Vista Programs.

A] True

B] False

Q.29. What is "Windows Aero"

A] It is the graphical user interface for Windows XP.

B] It is the graphical user interface for Windows Vista.

C] Application Program

D] None of these

Q.30. Which is the basic program of a computer?

A] Operating System

B] Software Program

C] Application Program

D] None of these

Q.31. As you type, the text automatically moves to the next line it reaches the right end of the margin. This feature is called "Word Wrap."

A] True

B] False

Q.32. "Log Off" is a power-saving state.

A] True

B] False

Q.33. In windows vista, you can see multiple programs running simultaneously on different areas of your screen.

A] True

B] False

Q.34. The .... Menu is used to enhance the appearance of the contained presented in a document.

A] "Insert"

B] "Edit" ?

C] "Format"

D] "File"

Q.35. The "text" tool is used to add text to a paint object.

A] True

B] False

Q.36. "............." helps in guarding your computer against malicious software.

A] "Windows Firewall"

B] "Windows Defender"

C] "Spy ware"

D] of these.

Q.37. .... is a basic text editing programme and it is most commonly used to view or edit text files.

A] "Calculator"

B] "Notepad"

C] "Address book"

D] "Paint"

Q.38. In a windows operating system screen saver

A] is helps in guarding your computer against many types of malicious software.

B] is a long, vertical bar that is displayed on the side of your desktop.

C] is a programme that displays on image, animation, or just a blank screen on a Computer after on input has been received for a certain length of time.

D] None of these.

Q.39. Features in Windows Vista make it easier, safer and more entertaining to use your PC virtually anytime and anywhere.

A] True

B] False

Q.40. The programmes on the .... in Windows Vista remain there and are always available for you to click to start them.

A] the "Most frequently use programmes list.

B] "pinned items list"

C] "Documents"

D] "Control Panel"

Q.41. In Windows Vista .... is a power-saving state.

A] Log off

B] Sleep

C] Restart

D] Lock

Q.42. AERO is an abbreviation of ....

A] Authentic, Energetic, Reflective and Open.

B] Essential, Reflective and Open.

C] Arithmetic, Essential, Reflective and Object.

D] Authentic, Essential, Reflective and Open.

Q.43. At the bottom of the screen, you can see a long, thin bar which is called as ....

A] "Task bar"

B] "Title bar"

C] "Menu bar"

D] "Spacebar"

Q.44. In Windows Vista a "Clipboard" is ....

A] an application program

B] a temporary storage area for information that you have copied or moved from one place and plan to use somewhere else.

C] an operating system.

D] None of these.

Q.45. .... is a basic text editing programme and it is most commonly used to view or edit text files.

A] "Calculator"

B] "Notepad"

C] "Address book"

D] "Paint"

Q.46. ...., is a drawing programme that can be used to create modify graphic images.

A] "Brush"

B] "Paint"

C] "Notepad"

D] "WordPad"

Q.47. The .... menu is used to enhance the apperance of the content presented in a document.

A] "Insert"

B] "Edit"

C] "Format"

D] "File"

Q.48. A .... is a rectangular section on the screen that is used to display information and other programme.

A] Icon

B] Desktop

C] Window

D] Panel

Q.49. The capability of an operating system to run multiple programmes at the same time is called "Multitasking."

A] True

B] False

Q.50. In Window vista, you can see multiple Programme running simultaneously on different areas of your screen

A]True

B] False

Q.51. The name of a file consist of two parts

A] Folder Name

B] use Extension

C] File Name

D] use Sub folder Name

Q.52. We can navigate through text using

A] Cpu

B] Mouse

C] Key board

D] Monitor

Q.1. In MS Word 2007 when text is selected, a "..........." is automatically displayed.

A] Taskbar

B] Main Toolbar

C] Mini Toolbar

D] Menu bar

Q.2. You can make for a TOC using:

A] Heading styles.

B] Custom styles.

C] Outline levels.

D] All of these.

Q.3. .... contains command for opening, saving, printing and closing a file.

A] "Home"

B] "Office Button"

C] "View"

D] "Insert"

Q.4. .... offers a wide variety of options to design documents.

A] Microsoft Excel

B] Microsoft PowerPoint

C] Microsoft Word

D] Microsoft Access

Q.5. All of the following Ribbon tabs are displayed in Word 2007, EXCEPT

A] Home

B] Insert

C] Tools

D] Page Layout

Q.6. When you use the mouse to move the insertion point, the shape of mouse pointer is like I-beam.

A] True

B] False

Q.7. Index shows you at a glance, the topics that are included in the document and make it easier to locate information.

A] True

B] False

Q.8. You can click on the "Format" tab under "WordArt tools" to modify the WordArt as per your requirements.

A] True

B] False

Q.9. In Word, a file is called as a ....

A] "template"

B] "form"

C] "database"

D] "Document"

Q.10. The Mail Marge feature, combines a list of data, typically a file of names and addresses.

A]True

B] False

Q.11. Microsoft Word is the only word processor available in the market.

A] True

B] False

Q.12. Hyperlink identifies a location in the document or a section of text that you name for feature reference.

A] True

B] False

Q.13. A .... is a reference from one part of a document to related information in same another part.

A] Hyperlink

B] Cross-reference

C] Document

D] Linkage

Q.14. For Indentation you may use the "Decrease Indent" and "Increase Indent" icons in the "Paragraph" group on the "............" tab for indenting your text.

A] Insert

B] Home

C] Page Layout

D] Data

Q.15. In MS Word 2007 the "References" tab contains spell check, the squares, and track changes.

A] True

A] False

Q.16. The "..............." is a dictionary of synonyms which you can use to find words that are synonyms with a term.

A] Translate

B] Spelling

C] Thesaurus

D] Research

Q.17. A " .... " is a listing of the topics that appear in a document with their associated page references.

A] Index

B] Table

C] Clipboard

D] Table of contents

Q.18. You can format your document automatically applying styles, available in MS Word 2007.

A] True

B] False

Q.19. A "............." is a connection to a location in the current document to another document or Web Site.

A] Link

B] hyperlink

C] hypolink

D] linkage

Q.20. To view a document in the Print Preview Mode, click on the Office Button and select "Print Print Preview."

A] True

B] False

Q.21. You may use the "The Auto Complete Feature" to automatically correct the grammatical and spelling mistakes in your document.

A] True

B] False

Q.22. Using a word Processing application you can create, modify, store, retrieve and print a document.

A] True

B] False

Q.23. "Mini Toolbar" provides easy way to access the most frequently used formatting commands.

A] True

B] False

Q.24. To print only selected pages in your documnet, you may use either the "Current page" or "Page" option under "Print Range."

A] True

B] False

Q.25. MS Word 2007 when we click on the Office Button the "Edit" menu is displayed.

A] True

B] False

Q.26. A "................." is a pre-designed document useful for creating common purpose documents such as a fax, invoice or business letter.

A] Template

B] File

C] Form

D] Database

Q.27. A multileve list shows the list items at different levels rather then single level.

A] True

B] False

Q.28. A "............." is used to organize information into an easy-to-read format of horizontal rows and vertical columns.

A] Cell

B] Sheet

C] Box

D] Table

Q.29. To remove individual character at the left you may press "............".

A] Delete

B] Backspace

C] Enter

D] Spacebar

Q.30. When you click on "Format Printer" icon on the "Home" tab, you can see that your mouse pointer changes to a "............" icon.

A] paintbrush

B] I-beam

C] Arrow

D] 4-Way arrow

Q.31. You may create a new document using standard templates provided by Word by checking on a template name in the "New Document" window.

A] True

B] False

Q.32. MS Word's Mail Merge feature facilitates you to mail your document about special offers to a large number of people.

A] True

B] False

Q.33. When you move your mouse over a button, a .... is displayed. That provides a detailed description of what the button does.

A] Super-tooltip

B] Sub-tooltip

C] Info

D] Key-tip

Q.34. MS Word 2007 can quickly sort text, data or numbers ascending or descending order.

A] True

B] False

Q.35. .... Applications help you to create different types of written documents such as personal letters, from letters, brochures, faxes and even professional manuals.

A] Word Processor

B] Word Pad

C] Note Pad

D] None of these

Q.36. The "Mailings" tab contains the items required for mail merge.

A] True

B] False

Q.37. Word places footnotes at the end of each page and end notes at the end of documents.

A] True

B] False

Q.38. To remove the hyperlink while retaining the text, right - click on it and select "Remove Hyperlink."

A] True

B] False

Q.39. MS Word indicates formatting inconsistencies with a red wavy underline.

A] True

B] False

Q.40. To automatically correct the document, we use

A] The auto correct feature

B] The auto complete feature

C] Formatting

D] Building Blocks

Q.41. A "..............." is a common application for news paper columns.

A] News reading

B] News letter

C] News

D] News editor

Q.42. Personal letters, form letters, brochures, faxes and professional manuals can be using word processors.

A] True

B] False

Q.43. The set margins, select "Margins" from the "Page Setup" group on the "Page Layout" tab.

A] True

B] False

Q.44. Drop caps are the first characters at the beginning of a paragraph that are enlarged, conversing several lines.

A] True

B] False

Q.45. A multilevel list shows the list items at different levels rather than single level.

A] True

B] False

Q.46. The "Page Layout" tab contains margin, orientation, and spacing properties.

A] True

B] False

Q.47. A "............" is used to mark a certain location in a document.

A] Index

B] Hyperlink

C] Bookmark

D] Table

Q.48. You may click on "Replace All" button to replace all occurrences of the search text by specified new text.

A] True

B] False

Q.49. While working on a document in MS Word 2007 when we click on the picture, it is surrounded by eight boxes called "Sizing handles" which is used to to change the size of the graphic.

A] True

B] False

Q.50. While changing the level of an item in hierarchy you can increase the indent by using

A] "Tab"

B] "Backspace"

C] "Delete"

D] "Spacebar"

Q.51. Footnotes or Endnotes are used to provide certain "........................".

A] References

B] Information

C] Points

D] Lists

Q.52. If you want the data to be automatically get updated in a document when the current data changes, check the "Update automatically" box.

A] True

B] False

Q.1. In formula bar, an adjacent range is specified by giving the starting and editing cell addresses separated by a

A] Semicolon

B] Comma

C] Full stop

D] Colon

Q.2. The cell address is displayed in the "Text Box".

A] True

B] False

Q.3. A .... is a visual representation of data and conveys the information in an easy to understand and attractive manner.

A] chart

B] table

C] picture

D] graphic

Q.4. In formulas, a non-adjacent range is specified by giving the cell addresses separated by a ....

A] Scmicolon

B] Comma

C] Full stop

D] Colon

Q.5. You can use the .... to enter and edit data, instead of editing directly in your work sheet.

A] formula bar

B] title bar

C] menu bar

D] space bar

Q.6. Your Excel 2007 file is stored with the extension "............".

A] ".docx"

B] ".xlsx"

C] ".xltx"

D] ".zltx"

Q.7. In an electronic spreadsheet or worksheet, data can be edited, new data can be added, and unwnated data can be deleted.

A] True

B] False

Q.8. The "Review" tab contains proofing tools like spell check & also has button that let you add comments to a worksheet and manage revisions.

A] True

B] False

Q.9. The "............" tab contains proofing tools like spell check.

A] "Review"

B] "Data"

C] "View"

D] "Insert"

Q.10. You can create and design our own work book templates.

A] True

B] False

Q.11. In a spreadsheet programme as you move from one cell to another, the reference or address to the active cell appears in the "Name Box."

A] True

B] False

Q.12. To start the Microsoft Excel Application, click on the "Start" button and select "All programmes Microsoft Office ? Microsoft Office Excel 2007.

A] True

B] False

Q.13. The "Insert" tab lets you add special ingredients like tables, graphics, charts, and hyperlinks in a spreadsheets programme.

A] True

B] False

Q.14. The text that appears in the bottom margin of the page is called as the "Footer".

A] True

B] False

Q.15. In Excel, a formula always begins with an equal sign] =. and uses arithmetic operators like +, -, *, /, %, and ^ to perform addition, subtraction, multiplication, division, percent and exponentiation respectively.

A] True

B] False

Q.16. While working you may have to reference data from more than one sheet which is called referencing multiple sheets.

A] True

B] False

Q.17. The defalut page orientation setting is "Landscape".

A] True

B] False

Q.18. "............." is a method which aids you in forecasting values.

A] "Find"

B] "Replace"

C] "Goal Seek"

D] "Go to"

Q.19. In MS Excel 2007, below the "Ribbon", we can see Name Box on the left and the Formula Bar on the right.

A] True

B] False

Q.20. A "..............." is a prewritten formula the performs calculations automatically.

A] "Function"

B] "Equation"

C] "Template"

D] "Reaction"

Q.21. MS Excel 2007 is used for different types of .... varying from vary simple to complex.

A] calculations

B] manipulations

C] presentations

D] expressions

Q.22. Your excel file is stored with the extension ".xltx".

A] True

B] False

Q.23. "Autocorrect" is a feature of Microsoft Excel 2007 that makes entering a series of heading easier by logically repeating and extending the series.

A] True

B] False

Q.24. "A relative reference" is a cell or range reference used in a formula whose location does not change when a formula is copied.

A] True

B] False

Q.25. While changing the level of an item in the hierarchy you can increase the indent by using.

A] "Tab"

B] "Backspace"

C] "Delete"

D] "Spacebar"

Q.26. To set margins, select "Margins" from the "Page Setup" group on the "Page Layout" tab.

A] True

B] False

Q.27. To remove individual character at the left you may press "..............".

A] Delete

B] Backspace

C] Enter

D] Spacebar

Q.28. Drop caps are the first character/s at the beginning that are enlarged, conversing several lines.

A] True

B] False

Q.29. The intersection of a row and a column is called a "................".

A] Table

B] Cell

C] Data

D] Sheet

Q.30. A .... is a file that is provided by the application in a "ready to use" format.

A] Sheet

B] Template

C] Book

D] Report

Q.31. A .... is a visual representation of data and conveys the information in a easy to understand and attractive manner.

A] Chart

B] Table

C] Picture

D] Graphic

Q.32. To move among the worksheet in your workbook, you need to click on the "Workbook" tab.

A] True

B] False

Q.33. A theme comprise of a colour palette, font set, and effects.

A] True

B] False

Q.34. You can view two areas of worksheet and lock rows or columns in one area by splitting or freezing panes.

A] True

B] False

Q.35. "............" are individual designs that can be applied to different parts to the document.

A] "Graphics"

B] "Styles"

C] "Pictures"

D] "Themes"

Q.36. "............" contains commands for opening, saving, printing, and closing a file.

A] "View" tab

B] "Office Button"

C] "Insert" tab

D] "Review" tab

Q.37. When a formula containing an absolute cell reference is copied to another row or column in the worksheet, the cell reference does not change.

A] True

B] False

Q.38. The "header" is usually the title you give on the page.

A] True

B] False

Q.39. The text that appears in the top margin of the page is called the ....

A] Footer

B] Column

C] Header

D] Paragraph

Q.40. In a spreadsheet programme a table is a selection of two or more cells.

A] True

B] False

Q.41. The "title" is usually given as the footer.

A] True

B] False

Q.42. To stop the automatic relative cell references, i.e. to make the cell reference absolute, type a .... character before the column and row number.

A] # hash.

B] $ dollar.

C] % percent.

D] * star.

Q.43. A theme comprise of a colour palette, font set, and effects.

A] True

B] False

Q.44. To select a group or range of cells, click on the cell you want to begin, drag your cursor and release it when you have reached the end of the selection.

A] True

B] False

Q.45. If we require to add more data to be on one page, we change the page orientation to land scape.

A] True

B] False

Q.46. Each worksheet can be used to organized different types of related information.

A] True

B] False

Q.47. The "table" is a visual representation of data and convey the information in an easy to understand and attractive manner.

A] True

B] False

Q.48. "Themes" provided with MS Excel 2007 are universal designs that unify all of the styles.

A] True

B] False

Q.49. In Microsoft Excel 2007, a single file or document is called a "............".

A] Workbook

B] Worksheet

C] Sheet

D] Notebook

Q.50. "Notebook" contains a collection of one or more worksheets and, optionally, chart sheets containing graphic pictures of your worksheet data.

A] True

B] False

Q.51. With the .... option, you can freeze either or both, rows and columns ie. regardless of where you are in the worksheet you can see the information in these rows and/or columns at all times.

A] Split

B] Arrange

C] Fitter

D] Freeze Panes

Q.52. You can create charts to represent data more effectively in an electronic sheet or worksheet.

A] True

B] False

Q.53. In a spreadsheet each cell has its own address called as "cell address".

A] True

B] False

Q.54. A template file in MS Excel 2007 has an extension "................".

A] .docx

B] .yltx

C] .xltx

D] .zltx

Q.55. A "............" is like an accountant's ledger consisting of rows and columns.

A] Table

B] Microsoft Excel 2007

C] Format

D] Sheet

Q.56. A "table" is a visual representation of data and conveys the information in an easy to understand and attractive manner.

A] True

B] False

Q.1. The "Insert" tab contains the basic set of objects which you can insert into a slide.

A] True

B] False

Q.2. Click "Replace All" to replace all occurrences of search text by the specified new text.

A] True

B] False

Q.3. A "................" graphic is a visual representation of your information and ideas.

A] "WordArt"

B] "ClipArt"

C] "SmartArt"

D] "Autoshape"

Q.4. To start a Microsoft PowerPoint Application, click on the "Start" button and select "All progrmmes ? Microsoft Office ? Microsoft Office PowerPoint 2007".

A] True

B] False

Q.5. "..............." refer to a ready-to-use picture.

A] "WordArt"

B] "ClipArt"

C] "SmartArt"

D] "Autoshape"

Q.6. To open a recently used presentation you may click the office button and then click on the presentation name in the list displayed under "Recent Documents".

A] True

B] False

Q.7. SmartArt programs are designed to help you to create an effective presentation.

A] True

B] False

Q.8. The "............." tab contains tools that controls how to slide show is presented.

A] "Design"

B] "Slide Show"

C] "Review"

D] "View"

Q.9. Minature pictures of slides displayed in the slide sorter view.

A] True

B] False

Q.10. .... which displays icon that represent commonly used commands such as Save, Undo, and Redo.

A] Home Button

B] The Ribbon

C] The Quick Access Tool bar

D] The Office Button

Q.11. A "..........." is a connection to a location in the current documnet, another document or a website.

A] Highlink

B] hipolink

C] linkage

D] hyperlink

Q.12. .... are used to create slide shows on the computer

A] Presentation graphics

B] Analytical development programs

C] Super Slide packages

D] Slide maker tools

Q.13. To preview your presentation as web page, you need to add the "Web Page Preview" command to Ribbon.

A] True

B] False

Q.14. With "Slide Show View" you can see how your graphics timings, movies, animated elements and transition effects will look in the actulashow.

A] True

B] False

Q.15. In graphic presentation, programmes each presentation is divided into ....

A] charts

B] slides

C] tables

D] pictures

Q.16. In PowerPoint "Match case": you may check this box for a case sensitive search.

A] True

B] False

Q.17. "Scale to fit paper": check this box to print the slides with an outer frame.

A] True

B] False

Q.18. In PowerPoint "build effects" are animations to slide contents..

A] True

B] False

Q.19. A "..............." is a pre-designed presentation designed for common purpose such as photo album or a quiz show.

A] "Chart"

B] "Table"

C] "Slide"

D] "Template"

Q.20. You may create a new presentation using a template provided by PowerPoint.

A] True

B] False

Q.21. We can insert a video clip on a PowerPoint Slide.

A] True

B] False

Q.22. When you move your mouse over a sizing handle the pointer becomes a ".............".

A] Round Arrow

B] Two-headed Arrow

C] Plus Sign

D] Four-headed Arrow

Q.23. PowerPoint Presentation is a component of following application software.

A] Leap Office

B] Start Office

C] Open Office

D] MS Office

Q.24. "Slide Show View" is an exclusive view of your slides in thumbnail form.

A] True

B] False

Q.25. Headers and Footers are used to add information such as slide numbers, the time and date, a company logo or the presentation title to the top of a hand out or notes page in your presentation, or to bottom of a slide, handout or notes page.

A] True

B] False

Q.26. To see a preview of your slide in a window on the screen, click on the Quick Access Toolbar and select "Print ? Print Preview".

A] True

B] <u>False</u>

Q.27. In Graphics Presentation Programs each presentation is divided into charts.

A] True

B] <u>False</u>

Q.28. Using WordArt graphics, you can effectively communicate your message in a quick and msimple way.

A] True

B] <u>False</u>

Q.29. You may change the presentation views by checking on the buttons displayed on the "..........." at the bottom of the screen.

A] "Title bar"

B] "Menu bar"

C] "Tool bar"

D] <u>"Status bar"</u>

Q.30. "Animations" refers to addition of special visual or sound effect to your slides.

A] <u>True</u>

B] False

Q.31. Using PowerPoint presentation graphics is simple and it is used for effective presentation

A] on a topic.

B] <u>True</u>

C] False

Q.32. A "review" is a way to looking at a presentation.

A] True

B] <u>False</u>

Q.33. In Presentation Graphics "..........." are used to add information such as slide numbers, the time and date, a company logo or the presentation title to the top of a handout or notes page in your presentation, or a bottom of a slide, handout or notes.

A] Hyperlinks

B] Tables

C] <u>Header and Footers</u>

D] Charts

Q.34. The sizing handles at the slides are used to adjust only the height or the width.

A] <u>True</u>

B] False

Q.35. "..............." takes up the full computer screen, like an actual slide show presentation.

A] Slide Sorter View

B] Normal View

C] Slide Show View

D] Notes Page

Q.36. The "Outline" tab shows your slide text in outline form.

A] True

B] False

Q.37. A slide layout refers to the arrangements of elements, such as text, pictures, tables, charts and movies, on a slide.

A] True

B] False

Q.38. If you have a large number of slides in your presentation, you may find it more convenient to use the .... to view all your slides and change their positions.

A] Normal View

B] Slide Sorter View

C] Slide Show View

D] Notes Page

Q.39. You may use either the Normal View or the Slide Sorter View to delete a Slide.

A] True

B] False

Q.40. In Microsoft PowerPoint your file is stored with the .... extension.

A] psd

B] .rtf

C] .pptx

D] .docx

Q.41. When the pointer becomes a ...., you can drag placeholder to the location you wish.

A] Round arrow

B] Two-round arrow

C] Plus sign

D] Four-headed arrow

Q.42. A "Clip" may be a single media file, including art, sound, animation or movies.

A] True

B] False

Q.43. "............" are details about a file that help identify it.

A] Desktop Properties

B] Window Properties

C] Advanced Properties

D] Document Properties

Q.44. The "Sizing Handles" at the slides and corners of the selection rectangle can be used to adjust the size of the place holder.

A] True

B] False

Q.45. To open a file that you have previously saved, click the Ribbon and select "Open".

A] True

B] False

Q.46. ".............." is the main editing view.

A] Slide Sorter View

B] Normal View

C] Slide Show View

D] Notes Page

Q.47. We can insert a audio clip on a powerpoint slide.

A] True

B] False

Q.48. In PowerPoint the “Insert” tab contains tools to design your slides.

A] True

B] False

Q.49. The “...........” tab contains the basic formatting tools.

A] “Design”

B] “View”

C] “Insert”

D] ”Home”

Q.50. The “Slides” tab makes it easy to navigate through your presentation and to see the effects of changes and also rearrange, add or delete sliders.

A] True

B] False

Q.51. The “Outline” tab shows you slides as your thumbnail sized images while you edit.

A] True

B] False

Q.52. In PowerPoint the “Insert” tab contains tools to design your slides.

A] True

B] False

Q.1. You can start the name of the field with a space.

A] True.

B] False.

Q.2. "............." is a database object that is mainly used to enter and display records and make changes to existing records on screens.

A] query.

B] form.

C] report.

D] table.

Q.3. Primary Number is a unique, sequential number that is automatically incremented by one whenever a new record is added to the table.

A] True.

B] False.

Q.4. each column is a record which is the smallest unit of information about a record.

A] True.

B] False.

Q.5. A form is a printed output generated from tables and queries.

A] True.

B] False.

Q.6. The ribbon has Task-oriented Tabs, Groups and command buttons.

A] True.

B] False.

Q.7. "............." is an electronic database management system which can store, organize access, manipulate, and present information in many different ways.

A] MS Access 2007.

B] MS Word.

C] MS Excel.

D] MS PowerPoint.

Q.8. A professional database is the most widely used database structure.

A] True.

B] False.

Q.9. The tables are related or linked to one another by a common field.

A] True.

B] False.

Q.10. When you select a data type, its default properties are displayed under "Display Properties."

A] True.

B] False.

Q.11. "............." data type is used to store numbers only.

A] Auto Number.

B] Text.

C] Number.

D] Date/Time.

Q.12. A default value is used to specify a value that is automatically entered in a field when a new record is added.

A] True.

B] False.

Q.13. "..........." stores the information in Access 2007.

A] Table.

B] Queries.

C] Reports.

D] Forms.

Q.14. A field property is a characteristic that helps to define a field.

A] True.

B] False.

Q.15. ".........." data type is used to store images, documents, graphs etc.

A] Hyperlink.

B] OEL Object.

C] Text.

D] Description.

Q.16. ".........." decides the maximum number of characters that can be entered in the field.

A] Format.

B] Input Mask.

C] Caption.

D] Field Size.

Q.17. The information in a database is stored in a ....

A] Chart.

B] Box.

C] Folder.

D] Table.

Q.18. "............" is the default data type and is used to store text entries like words, combinations of words and numbers and numbers that are not used in calculations.

A] Text.

B] Number.

C] Memo.

D] Currency.

Q.19. In Access, you can sort data in ascending or descending order.

A] True.

B] False.

Q.20. Access provides different window formats called "Lists" to display and work with the objects in a database.

A] True.

B] False.

Q.21. In Access, every database is stored in a single file which has the extension.

A] ".docx"

B] ".rtf"

C] ".accdb"

D] ".txt"

Q.22. The data type defines the type of data the field will contain.

A] True.

B] False.

Q.23. A .... is used to identify the data stored in a field.

A] Table.

B] Field Name.

C] Box.

D] Bracket.

Q.24. A database is an organized collection of related information.

A] True.

B] False.

Q.25. ".........." simplifies data entry and controls what data is required and how it is to be displayed.

A] Format.

B] Input Mask.

C] Caption.

D] Field Size.

Q.26. Access automatically creates a code for the primary key, which helps makes queries and other operations.

A] True.

B] False.

Q.27. .... provides a number of data types.

A] Word 2007.

B] Access 2007.

C] Excel 2007.

D] PowerPoint 2007.

Q.28. It is difficult to add, delete and modify records from a table.

A] True.

B] False.

Q.29. The "Form Wizard" feature of Access 2007 makes it very easy to design forms.

A] True.

B] False.

Q.30. When you open a database or create a new one, the names of your database objects such a tables. Forms and reports appear in the Navigation Pane.

A] True.

B] False.

Q.31. Charts are made up of vertical columns] called fields. and horizontal rows] called records.

A] True.

B] False.

Q.32. You can quickly produce reports using some MS Access features.

A] True.

B] False.

Q.33."..........." are windows that you create and arrange in order to easily view or change the information in a table.

A] Table.

B] Queries.

C] Report.

D] Forms.

Q.34. "........." restricts the data easy to meet certain conditions or requirements.

A] Validation Text.

B] Default Value.

C] Validation Rule.

D] Format.

Q.35. Forms help you print same or all of the information in a table.

A] True.

B] False.

Q.36. ".........." data type is used to store text that is too long to be stored in a text field.

A] Text.

B] Number.

C] Memo.

D] Currency.

Q.37. The "Description" text box is used to describe the field.

A] True.

B] False.

Q.38. "..........." specifies a field caption or a prompt for the user to enter data.

A] Format.

B] Input Mask.

C] Caption.

D] Field Size.

Q.39. "Form Wizard" guides you through the steps required to create a form.

A] True.

B] False.

Q.40. A field name is to identify the data stored in a field.

A] True.

B] False.

Q.41. A default value is an expression that defines acceptable values.

A] True.

B] False.

Q.42. Each row is a field which contains all the information about a person, thing or place.

A] True.

B] False.

Q.43. A primary key must be

A] Unique But Permit Null.

B] Unique and Not Null.

C] Non-unique And Not Null.

D] Non-unique And Permit Null.

Q.44. which of the following are functions performed by a DBA?

A] Database Design.

B] System Security.

C] Backup and Recovery.

D] All of the above.

Q.45. "..........." is a relation database management application that is used to create and analyze a database.

A] Word 2007.

B] Access 2007.

C] System Security.

D] PowerPoint 2007.

Q.46. You can create as many tables as you need to store different types of information.

A] True.

B] False.

Q.47. A "............" is a field or set of fields in your table that provide Access with a unique identifier for every record.

A] Password.

B] Special Code.

C] Primary Key.

D] Unique Code.

Q.48. The photo can be inserted as a file.

A] True.

B] False.

Q.49. You can analyze the data in a table and perform calculations on different fields of data.

A] True.

B] False.

Q.50. Formatting the data often helps in finding some particular information quickly.

A] True.

B] False.

Q.51. what is the first step of defining a database.

A] Designing the database.

B] Collection of data.

C] Planning your database.

D] Digitizing your data.

Q.52. The "Print Preview" tab appears when you view the table in the print preview mode.

A] True.

B] False.

Q.53. Datasheet view can be used to create and view the design of all types of database objects such as tables, forms, queries, and reports.

A] True.

B] False.

Q.54. DBMS means..................

A] Database Management System.

B] Domain Management System.

C] Domain Manangeemt Server.

D] Domain Management Style.

Q.55. Access also ensure that every record has a non-blank primary key field, and that it is always unique.

A] True.

B] False.

Q.56. “Validation Rule” specifies a default value for a field to be automatically field n at the time of data entry.

A] True.

B] False.

Q.57. Design view provides a row and column view of the data in tables, forms, and queries.

A] True.

B] False.

Q.58 You can enter up to charactess in a text field.

A] 375

B] 125

C] 235

D] 255

Q.1. Netscape Navigator is a type of ....

A] Utility Program.

B] Operating System.

C] Browser.

D] Web Authoring Program.

Q.2. When you type an address such as "http://www.mkcl.org", in this .org indicates.

A] Original Web Site.

B] Commercial Web Site.

C] Organizational Web Site.

D] Educational Web Site.

Q.3. You can search the World Wide Web for a specific topic by using .... and.................

A] Gophers, Fido's.

B] Scanner, Search Engine.

C] Search Engines, Indexes.

D Browsers, Larkers.

Q.4. A] n. .... is a set of rules for how information and messages are sent over the internet.

A] Protocol.

B] ISP.

C] Applet.

D] HTML Hyper Text Markup Language.

Q.5. Discussion on the internet about specific topic is known as

A] News.

B] News group.

C] Veronica.

D] Telnet.

Q.6. Which of the following is not a type of protocol?

A] TCI/IP

B] ASCII

C] None of these.

D] ppp

Q.7. Which of the following is a type of protocol?

A] ASCII

B] RAM

C] TCI/IP

D] DBA

Q.8. The three parts of an e-mail message are

A] TCP/IP, Domain and ISP.

B] Destination, Device and Sender.

C] Header, Message and Signature.

D] TCP, IP and Message.

Q.9. The network connecting several computers all over the world is?

A] Intranet.

B] Internet.

C] Arpanet.

D] Network.

Q.10. Which of the following is a browser.

A] Web site.

B] Microsoft.

C] Internet Explorer.

D] www.

Q.11. The terms DNS stands for.

A] Data Naming System.

B] Do Name System.

C] Domain Name System.

D] Duplicate Name System.

Q.12. Internet e-mail address is .... for every user.

A] Unique.

B] Same.

C] Common.

D] None of these.

Q.13. For navigating any website, user has to enter

A] URL.

B] www.

C] PPP.

D] None of these.

Q.14. What is the full form of E-Commerce ?

A] English Commerce.

B] Electronic Commerce.

C] Electric Commerce.

D] Element Commerce.

Q.15. To send e-mail to someone you need ....

A] Resident Address.

B] Internet Connectivity.

C] Fax Address.

D] None of these.

Q.16. .... is used to see the web page.

A] Inbox.

B] Recycle bin.
C] Internet Explorer.
D] Network Neighbourhood.
Q.17. Full form of URL
A] Universal Resource Locator.
B] Uniform Resource Locator.
C] Uni Resource Locator.
D] None of these.
Q.18. Modem converts data from a CD to a hard disk.
A] True.
B] False.
Q.19. Which of the following is a search engine.
A] Google.
B] Alta Vista.
C] Yahoo.
D] All of these.
Q.20. What is meant by E-Commerce?
A] Online selling, purchasing, account handling etc.
B] Subject commerce stream.
C] Electronic equipment to deal with commercial problem.
D] All of the above.
Q.21. . The extensions .gov, .edu, .mil, and .net are called.
A] DNSs.
B] E-mail targets.
C] Domain codes.
D] Mail to address.
Q.22. Web spiders and crawlers are examples of
A] Browsers.
B] Search Engines.
C] HTML Programs.
D] Flames.
Q.23. What is an URL ?
A] A software package used to cruise the World Wide Web..
B] The address of a resource on the World Wide Web.
C] The terms used to describe an internal wizard.
D] A live chat program [Unlimited real time language.
Q.24. What does the abbreviation "www." stands for.
A] World Wide Web.

B] Wide Wide Web.

C] World Width Web.

D] World with Web.

Q.25. Website that allows the user to search for data on keywords is:

A] Chat engines.

B] Routers.

C] Web Server.

D] Search engines.

Q.26. Which of the following web search engine is used worldwide?

A] Domain.

B] Google.

C] Toggle.

D] None of these.

Q.27. When you use a(n) .... to search for a topic, the information you search through is organized into a database like structure.

A] Search engine.

B] Index.

C] Spider.

D] Applet.

Q.28. Which of the following system electronic letter or message sent between individuals or computers.

A] E-mail.

B] Online Service.

C] Share Resources.

D] Voice mail messaging.

Q.29. To add current web to the favourites list.

A] Click "Favourites - Add to Favourites".

B] Click "Add - Favourites.

C] Click "File - Favourites.

D] All of these.

Q.30. Moving around the web from one site to another is referred to as................

A] Linking.

B] Navigating.

C] Hopping.

D] Paging.

Q.31. A protocol defines the rules for passing information between two or more computers.

A] <u>True.</u>

B] False.

Q.32. Information sent over the Internet is divided into small pieces called.

A] <u>Packets.</u>

B] PPPs.

C] e-mail forms.

D] Messages.

Q.33. Protocols like PPP and SLIP are used for.

A] <u>Data Transfer.</u>

B] Dialup internet connection.

C] Domain Registration.

D] None of these.

Q.34. The .com indicates websites of............. Types of organization.

A] <u>Commercial.</u>

B] Complex.

C] Company.

D] Cargo.

Q.35. Sending messages on the internet to another person's mailbox is

A] E-Business.

B] E-Letter.

C] <u>E-Mail.</u>

D] Cyber Mali.

Q.1. This is a type of personal information managers.

A] MS Word 2007

B] MS Excel 2007

C] MS PowerPoint 2007

D] <u>MS Outlook 2007</u>

Q.2. You can attach all sorts of files to an e-mail including Spreadsheets, word processor document database, even sound recordings and graphic images.

A] <u>True</u>

B] False

Q.3. To create a mail, We click on "Mail in the navigation pane.

A] <u>True</u>

B] False

Q.4. You uses the "Send/Receive" button to Send and receive mails.

A] <u>True.</u>

B] False.

Q.5. If you want to personalize your work environments wish to use a tool that organizes your contacts. Schedules etc. You will use.

A] Microsoft Office Excel 2007

B] Microsoft Office PowerPoint 2007

C] Microsoft Office Outlook 2007

D] Microsoft Office Word 2007

Q.6. Entry in MS Outlook 2007, that losts for more than 24 hours is called as

A] Event

B] Exhibition

C] Mail

D] Calendar

Q.7. Creating a Mail massage is also known as "Consolidating" a mail.

A] True.

B] False.

Q.8. The most important feature of outlook 2007 is sending and receiving an e-mail.

A] True.

B] False.

Q.9. A .... is a descriptive keyboard or phrase used in MS Outlook 2007 in which you can assign related items.

A] Category

B] Mail

C] Notes

D] Point

Q.10. Sourting tasks are the process of rearranging items in ascending order.

A] True.

B] False.

Q.11. The "Notebook" is an electronic book. which includes detailed information of all the people with whom you communicate.

A] True.

B] False.

Q.12. .... are separate external files that are along with you e-mail message.

A] Attachments

B] Options

C] E-mails

D] Parcels

Q.13. A task is a personal work related action item.

A] True.

B] False.

Q.14. The "Instant Search" Feature helps you to quickly find items in Microsoft Office Outlook 2007.

A] True.

B] False.

Q.15. In MS Outlook 2007 you can update the status of the tasks at any time and specify and percentage completed.

A] True.

B] False.

Q.16. If you add a recipient's name using "BCC" the name is not Visible to other recipients of the message.

A] True.

B] False.

Q.17. When you start Microsoft Outlook 2007. All the mails that you receive gets deposited in your "Inbox" Folder as default.

A] True.

B] False.

Q.18. Once We click on the flag symbol next to an important mail it gets added in the To Do Bar.

A] True.

B] False.

Q.19. You may need to save your contacts to a file, so that are available for use in the future. This is called.................

A] "Saving"

B] "Importing"

C] "Exporting"

D] "Extracting"

Q.20. A Mailing list is a collection of contacts.

A] True.

B] False.

Q.21. To Forward that mail that you have received, click on the mail from the inbox and then click the "Forward" button.

A] True.

B] False.

Q.22. "Notes" are an electronic version of paper notes that you use to go down quick reminders.

A] <u>True</u>

B] False

Q.23. If you add a recipient's name using "Cc", the name is not visible to other recipients of the message.

A] True.

B] <u>False</u>.

Q.24. When you open Microsoft Outlook 2007, you will see a navigation pane on the left. Which contains catefories such as mail, calender and contacts etc?

A] <u>True</u>.

B] False.

Q.25. In the Tasks Timeline view in MS Outlook 2007. The tasks are arranged according to their due dates.

A] <u>True</u>.

B] False.

Q.26. Sorting "Categories" is the process of rearranging items in ascending or descending order.

A] True.

B] <u>False</u>.

Q.27. In MS Outlook 2007 you may add contacts form different books into your mailing list.

A] <u>True</u>.

B] False.

Q.28. When you went to convey the information that you have received to your friend or any other person you may .... the mail that you have received.

A] "Share"

B] "Give"

C] "Send"

D] <u>"Forward"</u>

Q.29. "Cc" stands for carbon copy and "Bcc" stands for blind carbon copy.

A] <u>True.</u>

B] False.

Q.30. The .... is an electronic book, which includes detailed information of all the people with whom you communicate.

A] Address book

B] Calendar

C] Task

D] Notebook

Q.31. You can use a flag to quickly create a follow-up item that can be tracked in the To-Do-Bar, in your Inbox, and even in he calendar.

A] True.

B] False.

Q.32. You can sort your tasks in MS Outlook 2007 according to subject by selecting "View Arrange By Subject".

A] True.

B] False.

Q.33. When you start Microsoft Outlook 2007, all the mails that you receive get deposited in your "Drafts" folder as default.

A] True.

B] False.

Q.1. When a web site is developed; the various interlinked files are grouped together. This is achieved using which facility.

A] Hypertext.

B] Hyperlinks.

C] Network.

D] None of these.

Q.2. What does the abbreviation "www" in internet stands for:

A] World Wide Web.

B] Wide Wide Web.

C] World Width Web.

D] World with Web.

Q.3. .... is one of the fastest growing internet applications.

A] E-mail.

B] Shopping.

C] Investing.

D] Commerce.

Q.4. .... is the new computer language used to write animation and games for the World Wide Web.

A] Java.

B] C.

C] C++.

D] HTML.

Q.5. .... Include mailing lists news groups and chat groups.

A] Discussion Groups.

B] Internet Groups.

C] IP Groups.

D] All of these.

Q.6. Which of the following is a search engine.

A] Google.

B] Alta Vista.

C] Yahoo.

D] All of these.

Q.7. Directory Search is also known as Index Search.

A] True.

B] False.

Q.8. In IRC, R stands for:

A] Real.

B] Relay.

C] Record.

D] Random.

Q.9. Applets are the special programs written in .... language.

A] Java.

B] HTML.

C] HTTP.

D] None of these.

Q.10. E-mail includes all of the following basic elements except.

A] Header.

B] Footer.

C] Message.

D] Signature.

Q.11. Instant messaging allows you

A] Send E-mail messages.

B] Sharing the data.

C] Instant reply of your messages.

D] To communicate with many at once in a conversation that occurs in real time.

Q.12.] When you use a] n. .... to search for a topic the information you search through is organized into a database - like structure.

A] Search Engine.

B] Index.

C] Spider.

D] Applet.

Q.13. .The extensions .gov, .edu, .mil, and .net are called.

A] DNSs.

B] E-mail targets.

C] Domain codes.

D] Mail to addresses.

Q.14.] Web spider are also known as search engines..

A] True.

B] False.

Q.15.B2c, C2C and B2B are types of...............

A] E-mail.

B] E-commerce.

C] E-cash.

D] All of these.

Q.16. For navigating any website, user has to enter.

A] URL.

B] www.

C] PPP.

D] None of these.

Q.17. Web spiders and Crawlers are examples of

A] Browsers.

B] Search Engines.

C] HTML Programs.

D] Flames.

Q.18. The .com indicates website of .... type of organization.

A] Commerce.

B] Complex.

C] Company.

D] Cargo.

Q.19.ISP stands for.

A] Internal Service Plan.

B] Internet Service Plan.

C] Integral Service Plan.

D] Internet Service Provider.

Q.20............ are programs that provide access to web resources.

A] Browsers.

B] Search Engines.

C] Programs.

D] All of these.

Q.21. Which is a web search engine used World Wide?

A] Domains.

B] Google.

C] Toggle.

D] All of these.

Q.22. Discussion on the internet about specific is known as

A] News.

B] News Group.

C] Veronica.

D] Telnet.

Q.23. Full from of URL

A] Universal Resource Locator.

B] Uniform Resource Locator.

C] Uni Resource Locator.

D] None of these.

Q.24. .... are the special programs written in Java.

A] Java Programs.

B] Applets.

C] Projects.

D] None of these.

Q.25. FTP stands for.

A] Field Transfer Project.

B] File Transfer Project.

C] File Transfer Protocol.

D] None of these.

Q.26. Plug-ins are programs that are automatically started and operate as a part of the browser.

A] True.

B] False.

Q.27. Keyword search is also known as Index search.

A] True.

B] False.

Q.28. When you type an address such as "http://www.mkcl.org," in this. org indicates that it is a

A] Original Web Site.

B] Commercial Web Site.

C] Organizational Web Site.

D] Educational Web Site.

Q.29. You can seach the World Wide Web for a specific topic by using .... and ....

A] Gophers, Fidos.

B] Scanners, Search engine.

C] Search engine, Index.

D] Browsers, Lukers.

Q.30. Mailing lists allow members to communicate by sending messages to a list address.

A] True.

B] False.

Q.31. A popular chat service is called -

A] Internet Release Chat.

B] Internet Request Chat.

C] Internet Resource Chat.

D] Internet Relay Chat.

Q.32. A programming language used for creating applets is called java.

A] True.

B] False.

Q.33. When you use a] n. .... to search for a topic, the information you search through is organized into a database - like structure.

A] Search Engine.

B] Index.

C] Spider.

D] Applet.

Q.34. The last part of the domain name following the dot .. is called as ....

A] Domain Codes.

B] E-mail Targets.

C] DNSs.

D] Mail to addresses.

Q.35. Following is a script language used, while designing a web page.

A] Hyper Text Mark-up Language.

B] Hyper Link Mark-up Language.

C] Hyper Text Web Language.

D] None of these.

Q.36. What is e-mail?

A] Engineering Mailing.

B] Internet Mailing.

C] Electronic Mailing.

D] All of the above.

Q.37. IM stands for ....

A] Instant Making.

B] Internal Messaging.

C] Instant Messaging.

D] None of these.

Q.38.Microsoft's internet explorel is awidely used browser.

A] True.

B] False.

Q.39. Directory search is also known as

A] Direct Search.

B] Unique Search.

C] Index Search.

D] All of these.

Q.40. What is URL

A] A software package used to cruise the World Wide Web.

B] The address of resource on the World Wide Web.

C] The term used to describe an internet wizard.

D] Unlimited Real time language.

Q.41. Netscape Navigator is a type of ....

A] Utility Program.

B] Operating System.

C] Browser.

D] Web Authoring Program.

Q.1........... Programs that guard your computer system against viruses or other damaging programs.

A] Backup.

B] Antivirus.

C] Uninstall.

D] None of these.

Q.2. Multitasking in the ability of the operating system to run more than one application at a time.

A] True.

B] False.

Q.3. .... is a utility program that locates and eliminates unnecessary fragments and rearranges files and unused disk space to optimize operations.

A] Backup.

B] Disk Defragmenter.

C] Uninstall.

D] All of these.

Q.4. Uninstall programs enable removing unneeded programs installed into the computer's hard disk.

A] True.

B] False.

Q.5. Backup programs make copies of the files to be used in case the original files are damaged or lost.

A] True.

B] False.

Q.6............ is the ability of the operating system to run more than one application at a time.

A] Booting.

B] Copping.

C] Pasting.

D] Multitasking.

Q.7............ are used to store data and programs.

A] Folder.

B] File.

C] Recycle bin.

D] None of these.

Q.8. A .... is a connecting ring.

A] Track.

B] Sectors.

C] Round.

D] None of these.

Q.9.The operating system provides the user interface, controls the computers resources, and runs programs.

A] True.

B] False.

Q.10. Each track is divided into wedge-shaped sections called ....

A] Track.

B] Sectors.

C] Round.

D] None of these.

Q.11............ are also known as service programs.

A] OS.

B] Device Drivers.

C] Utilities.

D] All of these.

Q.12. Type of software that can be described as "end user" software.

A] DOS.

B] System Software.

C] Application Software.

D] Operating Software.

Q.13.GUI Stands for

A] Graphical User Interface.

B] Greater User Interface.

C] Graphical Union Interface.

D] Graphical User Interface.

Q.14. Which of these operating system does not have a graphical user interface ?

A] Windows 95.

B] Mac OS.

C] Linux.

D] MS DOS.

Q.15. Language translators convert the programming instructions, written by programmers into a language that computer understand and process.

A] True.

B] False.

Q.16............ is a collection of several separate troubleshooting utilities.

A] Backup.

B] Norton Utilities.

C] Uninstall.

D] All of the above.

Q.17. .... provides the user interface, controls the computers resources, and runs programs.

A] Drivers.

B] Operating System.

C] Desktop.

D] None of these.

Q.18............ utility identifies non essential files on the hard disk and erases them only when user allows their erasure.

A] Uninstall Program.

B] Backup.

C] File Compression.

D] Disk Clean up.

Q.19. Which of the following is the function of operating system.

A] Managing Resources.

B] Running Applications.

C] Providing User Interface.

D] All of the Above.

Q.20. .... are graphical objects used to represent commonly used applications.

A] GUI.

B] Drivers.

C] Windows NT.

D] Icons.

Q.21. Starting or re-starting a computer is called............. The system.

A] Booting.

B] Copping.

C] Pasting.

D] Multitasking.

Q.22. .... are specialized programs that allow particular input or output devices to communicate with the rest of the computer system.

A] Device Drivers.

B] Utilities.

C] OS.

D] None of these.

Q.23. Disk Defragmenter is a utility program, that locates and eliminates unnecessary fragments and rearranges files and unused disk space to optimize operations.

A] True.

B] False.

Q.24. The .... displays a list of commands that can be used to gain access to information, change hardware settings, find information stored in the, get online help and shut down the computer.

A] GUI.

B] Desktop.

C] Icon.

D] Start Button.

Q.25. Which of the following example of network operating systems ?

A] Netware.

B] Windows N.T. Server.

C] Windows XP Server.

D] All of the above.

Q.26. Utilities are also known as service programs

A] True.

B] False.

Q.27. Which programs reduce the size of the files so that they occupy lesser space on the disk.

A] Backup.

B] Disk Cleanup.

C] File Compression.

D] Uninstall Program.

Q.28. Each track is divided into wedge-shaped called sectors.

A] True.

B] False.

Q.29. Starting or Restarting a computer is called multitasking the system.

A] True.

B] False.

Q.30. ………… convert the programming instruction written by programmers into a language that computers understand and process.

A] Utilities.

B] Device Drivers.

C] Language Translators.

D] None of these.

Q.31. System software includes all of the following except.

A] Operating System.

B] Device Drivers.

C] Utilities.

D] Desktop Publishing.

Q.32. ………… is background software that helps the computer manage its own internal resources.

A] System Software.

B] Information.

C] Objects.

D] None of these.

Q.33. Operating systems are programs that manage resource, provide user interface and run applications.

A] True.

B] False.

Q.34. Starting or Re-starting a computer is called booting the system.

A] True.

B] False.

Q.35. Antivirus programs are meant to guard a computer from invasion of the virus programs.

A] True.

B] False.

Q.36. Uninstall programs enable removing unneeded programs on started into

A] True.

B] False.

Q.37. Trouble shooting programs recognize both hardware and software problems and try to correct them as far as possible.

A] True.

B] False.

Q.38. Device Drivers are specialized programs that allow particular input or output devices to communicate with the rest computer system.

A] True.

B] False.

Q.39. Antivirus programs are meant to guard a computer from invasion of the virus programs.

A] True.

B] False.

Q.1. Microprocessor has two basic components.

A] Control Unit.

B] Arithmetic Logic Unit.

C] All of these.

D] None of these.

Q.2. Which of the following is a data processing unit

A] CPU.

B] RAM.

C] Hard Disk.

D] Floppy.

Q.3.Fire-Wire port is also called as High Performance Serial Bus HPSB. Port.

A] True.

B] False.

Q.4. Cache memory is used to store most frequently accessed information from the RAM.

A] True.

B] False.

Q.5. RISC stands for.

A] Reduced Instruction Set Computer.

B] Read Instruction Set Computer.

C] Reduce Instruction Software Computer.

D] None of these.

Q.6. The........... Connects all system computers and allows input and output device to communicate with the system unit.

A] System Board.

B] Monitor.

C] Mouse.

D] None of these.

Q.7. The types of microprocessor chips are

A] CISC Chips.

B] RISC Chips.

C] All of these.

D] None of these.

Q.8. Data transfer through a serial port is faster than that of a parallel port.

A] True.

B] False.

Q.9. Which of following is a primary memory ?

A] RAM.

B] CD.

C] Floppy.

D] Hard Disk.

Q.10. Random Access Memory] RAM. is .... type of memory.

A] Permanent.

B] Temporary.

C] Flash.

D] Smart.

Q.11. ASCII, EBCDIC and Unicode are examples of Application Software.

A] True.

B] False.

Q.12. Eight bits makes up a bite.

A] True.

B] False.

Q.13. In a microprocessor system, the Central Processing Unit C.P.U. Or a processor is contained on a single chip called the microprocessor.

A] True.

B] False.

Q.14. CISC stands for.

A] Computer Instruction Set Computer.

B] Complex Instruction Set Computer.

C] Complex Index Set Computer.

D] None of these.

Q.15. ASCII, EBCDIC and Unicode are binery coding schemes.

A] True.

B] False.

Q.16. Note book system units are often called as ....

A] PDA.

B] Laptop.

C] Desktop.

D] None of these.

Q.17. .... is also known as the system cabinet or chassis.

A] System Unit.

B] Monitor.

C] Key board.

D] None of these.

Q.18. Data stored in Flash RAM does not get erased even when power to the computer is switched off.

A] True.

B] False.

Q.19. The system board is also known as the main board or mother board.

A] True.

B] False.

Q.20. Capacity of a storage device is usually measured in terms of bytes.

A] True.

B] False.

Q.21. Which of the following component is used to store data?

A] CPU.

B] Memory.

C] Input Device.

D] Output Device.

Q.22. Microprocessor is often called a CPU.

A] True.

B] False.

Q.23. In a microprocessor system, the control processing unit] C.P.U.. or processor is contained on a single chip called the ....

A] Slot.

B] Port.

C] Microprocessor.

D] None of these.

Q.24. .... is a 16-bit code designed to support international language like Chinese and Japanese.

A] Unicode.

B] ASSCII

C] EBCDIC

D] None of these.

Q.26. Which of the following is the unit of computer memory.

A] Kilogram.

B] Kilobytes.

A] Meter.

B] Celsius.

Q.27. Parallel ports are mostly used to connect printers to the system unit.

A] True.

B] False.

Q.28. Data and instructions are represented electronically with a binary or two-state numbering system.

A] True.

B] False.

Q.29. Which of the following is the highest unit of memory ?

A] Gigabyte.

B] Bytes.

C] Megabytes.

D] Kilobytes.

Q.30. The system board connects all system components and allow input and output device to communicate with the system unit.

A] True.

B] False.

Q.31. In parallel port data is transmitted one byte after another.

A] True.

B] False.

Q.32. Which of the following is a primary memory?

A] RAM.

B] CD.

C] Floppy.

D] Hard Disk.

Q.33. Socrates, slots and bus lines are components of the system board.

A] True.

B] False.

Q.34. Each 0 and 1 in the binary numbering system is called a bit.

A] True.

B] False.

Q.1. Output of an image on the monitor screen is often called hard copy.

A] True.

B] False.

Q.2. MIRC can be used to read data from checks in a bank.

A] True.

B] False.

Q.3. A monitor with resolution of 800 x 600 has 800 pixels horizontally and 600 pixels vertically.

A] True.

B] False.

Q.4. The keys labelled 0 -9 on the keyboard are called.

A] Function Keys.

B] Typewriters Keys.

C] Numeric Keys.

D] Special purpose Keys.

Q.5. The functions of a mouse and a track ball are different.

A] True.

B] False.

Q.6. .... devices translate what people understand into a form that computers can process.

A] Input.

B] Output.

A] All of these.

B] None of these.

Q.7. The keyboards keys that are labelled F1, F2 and so on are called................

A] Function Keys.

B] Numeric Keys.

C] Typewriter Keys.

D] Special Purpose Key.

Q.8. Which of the following device is not from pointing type of device?

A] Mouse.

B] Touch screen.

C] Key board.

D] Joystick.

Q.9. which of these is not a input device?

A] Monitor.

B] Mouse.

C] Key board.

D] Joystick.

Q.10. OCR is used to translate printed text to machine readable code.

A] True.

B] False.

Q.11. Optical character recognition device and optical mark recognition device are two names of the same device.

A] True.

B] False.

Q.12. Aspect ratio of a monitor is the ratio of number of horizontal pixels to number of vertical pixels.

A] True.

B] False.

Q.13. Output of an image on the monitor screen is often called a hardcopy.

A] True.

B False.

Q.14. The keyboard keys like caps lock that turn a feature on or off are called.

A] Function Keys.

B] Combination Keys.

C] Toggle Keys.

D] Special Purpose Keys.

Q.15. Primary function of a monitor is to display information to the user.

A] True.

B] False.

Q.16. Headphone is a typical output device.

A] True.

B] False.

Q.17. The mouse pointer seen on the desktop is also called as...............

A] Arrow Pointer.

B] Key Pointer.

C] Display Pointer.

D] None of these.

Q.18. Plotters are used to produce special purpose graphics.

A] True.

B] False.

Q.19. Input device translate what people understand into a form that computers can process.

A] True.

B] False.

Q.20. Primary function of a common keyboard in a computer is to play music like a piano.

A] True.

B] False.

Q.21. The easiest way to access any part of the screen in the windows operating system is using the

A] Key board.

B] Rat.

C] Mouse.

D] Joystick.

Q.22. Dot matrix printers make irritating noise.

A] True.

B] False.

Q.23. Joystick is very useful in playing speed games.

A] True.

B] False.

Q.24. Printers can be connected to a computer for producing output on a paper.

A] True.

B] False.

Q.25. Instead of function keys which are use to create a shortcut.

A] Toggle Keys.

B] Special Keys.

C] Combination Keys.

D] Numeric Keys.

Q.26. Method of working of a flatbed scanner is mostly similar to a photocopying machine.

A] True.

B] False.

Q.27. Output of an image on the monitor screen is often called soft copy.

A] True.

B] False.

Q.28. Which printer print data or image by spraying small drops of ink at high speed into the surface of the paper ?

A] Ink Jet Printer.

B] Laser Printer.

C] Dot Matrix Printer.

D] Drum Printer.

Q.29. Which of the following key is not a toggle key ?

A] Caps Lock.

B] Num Lock.

C] Scroll Lock.

D] Control.

Q.30. The keyboard keys that have arrows on them are called.

A] Function Keys.

B] Navigation Keys.

C] Typewriters Keys.

D] Special Purpose Keys.

Q.31. A .... is a light sensitive pen like device.

A] Light Pen.

B] Joy Stick.

C] Touch Screen.

D] None of these.

Q.32. Output of an image through a printer is often called hard copy.

A] True.

B] False.

Q.33. which of the following device is used to play fast computer games?

A] Joystick.

B] Touch Surface.

C] Touch Screen.

D] Track Ball.

Q.1. A track on a disk is the one of the many circular ring shaped areas where data is written magnetically.

A] True.

B] False.

Q.2. Which of these is not a file compressing program ?

A] Win Zip.

B] PK Zip.

C] Win RAR.

D] RAID.

Q.3. The traditional floppy disk is the 1.44 MB 3.5 inch disk.

A] True.

B] False.

Q.4. .... disk from the Sony Corporation have a capacity of 200 MB or 720 MB.

A] Super Disk.

B] HiFD Disk.

C] Zip Disk.

D] None of these.

Q.5. High capacity disks also known as floppy disk cartridges are rapidly replacing the traditional floppy disk.

A] True.

B] False.

Q.6. .... improves hard-disk performance by anticipating data needs.

A] Disk Catching.

B] Disk Defragment.

C] Disk Writing.

D] None of these.

Q.7. 3.5 floppy disk capacity is ....

A] 1.44 MB.

B] 1 MB.

C] 1.66 MB.

D] 1.55 MB.

Q.8. Super disks are produced by Imation and have a 120 MB or 240 MB capacity.

A] True.

B] False.

Q.9. A CD-ROM stands for.

A] Compact Disk Read Only Memory.

B] Compact Disk Read Once Memory.

C] CD-RW.

D] None of these.

Q.10........... Programs that guard your computer system against viruses or other damaging programs.

A] Backup.

B] Anti Virus.

C] Uninstall.

D] None of these.

Q.11. What is the name given to a part of circle on which data is written in a storage media ?

A] Track.

B] Sector.

C] Cylinder.

D] Spiral.

Q.12. A CD-RW Disk means.

A] CD-Rewriteable.

B] CD-Recordable.

C] CD-ROM.

D] None of these.

Q.13. .... are produced by omega and topically have a 100 MB, 250 MB or 750 MB capacity over 500 times as much as today's standard floppy disk.

A] Super Disk.

B] HiFD Disk.

C] Zip Disk.

D] None of these.

Q.14. Primary storage is a volatile.

A] True.

B] False.

Q.15. HiFD Disks from the Sony Corporation have a capacity of 200 MB or 720 MB.

A] True.

B] False.

Q.16........... are produced by Imation and have a 120 MB or 240 MB capacity.

A] Super Disk.

B] HiFD Disk.

C] Zip Disk.

D] None of these.

Q.17. .... are removable storage devices used to store massive amounts of information.

A] Hard Disk Packs.

B] C.D..

C] Floppy Disk.

D] None of these.

Q.18. each track is divided into wedge-shaped sections called sectors.

A] True.

B] False.

Q.19. Storage device are hardware that reads data and programs from storage media.

A] True.

B] False.

Q.20. The 2 HD on a disk label means.

A] Two side, Low Density.

B] Two Side High Density.

C] One Side High Density.

D] None of these.

Q.21............ disks have a 120 MB storage capacity and the drivers are also able to read and store data on a standard 3.5" floppy disk.

A] Super Disks.

B] HiFD Disks.

C] Zip Disks.

D] None of these.

Q.22. Zip disks are produced by omega and typically have a 100 MB, 250 MB or 750 MB capacity over 500 times such as much as today's standard floppy disks.

A] True.

B] False.

Q.23. A CD-R stands for.

A] CD-Recordable.

B] CD-Runner.

C] CD-Receiver.

D] None of these.

Q.24. Each track is divided into wedge-shaped sections called.

A] Track.

B] Sectors.

C] Round.

D] None of these.

Q.25. Hard disk packs are removable storage devices used to massive amounts of information.

A] True.

B] False.

Q.26. Secondary Storage is non-volatile.

A] True.

B] False.

Q.27. Floppy disks are removable storage media.

A] True.

B] False.

1] Awebpage displays a picture] What tag was used to display that picture?

a] picture

b] image

c]img

d] src

2] <b> tag makes the enclosed text bold] What is other tag to make text bold?

a] <strong>

b] <dar>

c] <black>

d] <emp>

3] Tags and test that are not directly displayed on the page are written in ______ section]

a] <html>

b] <head>

c] <title>
d] <body>
4] Which tag inserts a line horizontally on your web page?
a] <hr>
b] <line>
c] <line direction="horizontal">
d] <tr>
5] What should be the first tag in any HTML document?
a] <head>
b] <title>
c] <html>
d] <document>
6] Which tag allows you to add a row in a table?
a] <td> and </td>
b] <cr> and </cr>
c] <th> and </th>
d] <tr> and </tr>
7] How can you make a bulleted list?
a] <list>
b] <nl>
c] <ul>
d] <ol>
8] How can you make a numbered list?
a] <dl>
b] <ol>
c] <list>
d] <ul>
9] How can you make an e-mail link?
a] <a href="xxx@yyy">
b] <mail href="xxx@yyy">
c] <mail>xxx@yyy</mail>
d] <a href="mailto:xxx@yyy">
10] What is the correct HTML for making a hyperlink?
a] <a href="http:// mcqsets]com">ICT Trends Quiz</a>
b] <a name="http://mcqsets]com">ICT Trends Quiz</a>
c] <http://mcqsets]com</a>
d] url="http://mcqsets]com">ICT Trends Quiz
11] Choose the correct HTML tag to make a text italic

a] <ii>
b] <italics>
c] <italic>
d] <i>
12] Choose the correct HTML tag to make a text bold?
a] <b>
b] <bold>
c] <bb>
d] <bld>
13] What is the correct HTML for adding a background color?
a] <body color="yellow">
b] <body bgcolor="yellow">
c] <background>yellow</background>
d] <body background="yellow">
14] Choose the correct HTML tag for the smallest size heading?
a] <heading>
b] <h6>
c] <h1>
d] <head>
15] What is the correct HTML tag for inserting a line break?
a]
b] <lb>
c] <break>
d] <newline>
16] What doesvlink attribute mean?
a] visited link
b] virtual link
c] very good link
d] active link
17] Which attribute is used to name an element uniquely?
a] class
b] id
c] dot
d] all of above
18] Which tag creates a check box for a form in HTML?
a] <checkbox>
b] <input type="checkbox">
c] <input=checkbox>

d] <input checkbox>

19] To create a combo box (drop down box) which tag will you use?

a] <select>

b] <list>

c] <input type="dropdown">

d] all of above

20] Which of the following is not a pair tag?

a] <p>

b] < u >

c] <i>

d] <img>

21] To create HTML document you requirea

a] web page editing software

b] High powered computer

c] Just a notepad can be used

d] None of above

22] The special formatting codes in HTML document used to present contentare

a] tags

b] attributes

c] values

d] None of above

23] HTML documents are saved in

a] Special binary format

b] Machine language codes

c] ASCII text

d] None of above

24] Some tags enclose the text] Those tags are known as

a] Couple tags

b] Single tags

c] Double tags

d] Pair tags

25] The _____ character tells browsers to stop tagging the text

a] ?

b] /

c] >

d] %

26] In HTML document the tags

a] Should be written in upper case
b] should be written in lower case
c] should be written in propercase
d] can be written in both uppercase or lowercase
27] Marquee is a tag in HTML to
a] mark the list of items to maintaininqueue
b] Mark the text so that it is hidden in browser
c] Display text with scrolling effect
d] None of above
28] There are _____ different of heading tags in HTML
a] 4
b] 5
c] 6
d] 7
29] To create a blank line in your web page
a] press Enter two times
b] press Shift + Enter
c] insert <BR> tag
d] insert <BLINE>
30] Which of the following is not a style tag?
a] <b>
b] <tt>
c] <i>
d] All of above are style tags
31] The way the browser displays the object can be modified by ______
a] attributes
b] parameters
c] modifiers
d] None of above
32] Which of the following HTML code is valid?
a] <font colour="red">
b] <font color="red">
c] <red><font>
d] All of above are style tags
33] Which of the following is an attribute related to font tag?
a] size
b] face
c] color

d] All of above are style tags

34] HTML supports

a] ordered lists

b] unordered lists

c] both type of lists

d] does not support those types

35] What tag is used to list individual items of an ordered list?

a] LI

b] OL

c] UL

d] None of above

36] When should you use path along with file name of picture in IMG tag?

a] path is optional and not necessary

b] when the location of image file andhtml file are different

c] when image file andhtml file both are on same location

d] path is always necessary when inserting image

37] Which of the following is not a valid alignment attribute?

a] Left

b] Right

c] Top

d] All of above

38] Which attribute is used withimg tag to display the text if image could not load in browser?

a] description

b] name

c] alt

d] id

39] Which attribute can be used with BODY tag to set background color green?

a] background="green"

b] bgcolor="green"

c] vlink="green"

d] None of above

40] Which attribute you'll use with TD tag to merge two cells horizontally?

a] merge=colspan2

b] rowspan=2

c] colspan=2
d] merge=row2

41] Awebpage displays a picture] What tag was used to display that picture?
a] picture
b]mage
c]img
d] src

42] <b> tag makes the enclosed text bold] What is other tag to make text bold?
a] <strong>
b] <dar>
c] <black>
d] <emp>

43] Tags and test that are not directly displayed on the page are written in ______ section]
a] <html>
b] <head>
c] <title>
d] <body>

44] Which tag inserts a line horizontally on your web page?
a] <hr>
b] <line>
c] <line direction="horizontal">
d] <tr>

45] What should be the first tag in any HTML document?
a] <head>
b] <title>
c] <html>
d] <document>

46] Which tag allows you to add a row in a table?
a] <td> and </td>
b] <cr> and </cr>
c] <th> and </th>
d] <tr> and </tr>

47] How can you make a bulleted list?
a] <list>
b] <nl>

c] <ul>
d] <ol>
48] How can you make a numbered list?
a] <dl>
b] <ol>
c] <list>
d] <ul>
49] How can you make an e-mail link?
a] <a href="xxx@yyy">
b] <mail href="xxx@yyy">
c] <mail>xxx@yyy</mail>
d] <a href="mailto:xxx@yyy">
50] What is the correct HTML for making a hyperlink?
a] <a href="http://mcqsets]com">MCQ Sets Quiz</a>
b] <a name="http://mcqsets]com">MCQ Sets Quiz</a>
c] <http://mcqsets]com</a>
d] url="http://mcqsets]com">MCQ Sets Quiz
1) CSS stands for -
A] Cascade style sheets
B] Color and style sheets
C] Cascading style sheets
D] None of the above
2) Which of the following is the correct syntax for referring the external style sheet?
A] <style src = example.css>
B] <style src = "example.css" >
C] <stylesheet> example.css </stylesheet>
D] <link rel="stylesheet" type="text/css" href="example.css">
3) The property in CSS used to change the background color of an element is -
A] bgcolor
B] color
C] background-color
D] All of the above
4) The property in CSS used to change the text color of an element is -
A] bgcolor
B] color
C] background-color

D] All of the above

Hide Answer Workspace

5) The CSS property used to control the element's font-size is -

A] text-style

B] text-size

C] font-size

D] None of the above

6) The HTML attribute used to define the inline styles is -

A] style

B] styles

C] class

D] None of the above

7) The HTML attribute used to define the internal stylesheet is -

A] <style>

B] style

C] <link>

D] <script>

8) Which of the following CSS property is used to set the background image of an element?

A] background-attachment

B] background-image

C] background-color

D] None of the above

9) Which of the following is the correct syntax to make the background-color of all paragraph elements to yellow?

A] p {background-color : yellow;}

B] p {background-color : #yellow;}

C] all {background-color : yellow;}

D] all p {background-color : #yellow;}

10) Which of the following is the correct syntax to display the hyperlinks without any underline?

A] a {text-decoration : underline;}

B] a {decoration : no-underline;}

C] a {text-decoration : none;}

D] None of the above

11) Which of the following property is used as the shorthand property for the padding properties?

A] padding-left

B] padding-right

C] padding

D] All of the above

12) The CSS property used to make the text bold is -

A] font-weight : bold

B] weight: bold

C] font: bold

D] style: bold

13) Are the negative values allowed in padding property?

A] Yes

B] No

C] Can't say

D] May be

14) Which of the following property is used as the shorthand property of margin properties?

A] margin-left

B] margin-right

C] margin

D] None of the above

15) The CSS property used to specify the transparency of an element is

-

A] opacity

B] filter

C] visibility

D] overlay

16) Which of the following is used to specify the subscript of text using CSS?

A] vertical-align: sub

B] vertical-align: super

C] vertical-align: subscript

D] of the above

17) Which of the following CSS property is used to specify the space between every letter inside an element?

A] alpha-spacing

B] character-spacing

C] letter-spacing

D] alphabet-spacing

18) The CSS property used to specify whether the text is written in the horizontal or vertical direction?

A] writing-mode

B] text-indent

C] word-break

D] None of the above

19) Which of the following syntax is correct in CSS to make each word of a sentence start with a capital letter?

A] text-style : capital;

B] transform : capitalize;

C] text-transform : capital;

D] text-transform : capitalize;

20) How to select the elements with the class name "example"?

A] example

B] #example

C] .example

D] Class example

21) Which of the following is the correct syntax to select all paragraph elements in a div element?

A] div p

B] p

C] div#p

D] div ~ p

22) Which of the following is the correct syntax to select the p siblings of a div element?

A] p

B] div + p

C] div p

D] div ~ p

23) The CSS property used to draw a line around the elements outside the border?

A] border

B] outline

C] padding

D] line

24) Which of the following CSS property is used to add shadows to the text?

A] text-shadow

B] text-stroke
C] text-overflow
D] text-decoration

25) Which of the following is not a value of the font-variant property in CSS?

A] normal
B] small-caps
C] large-caps
D] inherit

26) Which of the following CSS property is used to specify whether the table cells share the common or separate border?

A] border-collapse
B] border-radius
C] border-spacing
D] None of the above

27) The CSS property used to make the rounded borders, or rounded corners around an element is -

A] border-collapse
B] border-radius
C] border-spacing
D] None of the above

28) The CSS property used to set the distance between the borders of the adjacent cells in the table is -

A] border-collapse
B] border-radius
C] border-spacing
D] None of the above

29) Which of the following selector in CSS is used to select the elements that do not match the selectors?

A] :! selector
B] :not selector
C] :empty selector
D] None of the above

30) Which of the following is not a type of combinator?

A] >
B] ~
C] +
D] *

31) Which of the following CSS property defines how an image or video fits into container with established height and width?

A] object-fit

B] object-position

C] position

D] None of the above

32) Which type of CSS is used in the below code?

<p style = "border:2px solid red;">

A] Inline CSS

B] Internal CSS

C] External CSS

D] None of the above

33) Which of the following CSS property specifies the origin of the background-image?

A] background-origin

B] background-attachment

C] background-size

D] None of the above

34) The CSS property used to set the maximum width of the element's content box is -

A] max-width property

B] height property

C] max-height property

D] position property

35) Which if the following CSS function allows us to perform calculations?

A] calc() function

B] calculator() function

C] calculate() function

D] cal() function

36) The CSS property used to set the maximum height of the element's content box is -

A] max-width property

B] height property

C] max-height property

D] position property

37) The CSS property used to set the minimum width of the element's content box is -

A] max-width property

B] min-width property

C] width property

D] All of the above

38) Which of the following CSS property is used to represent the overflowed text which is not visible to the user?

A] text-shadow

B] text-stroke

C] text-overflow

D] text-decoration

39) The CSS property which is used to define the set the difference between two lines of your content is -

A] min-height property

B] max-height property

C] line-height property

D] None of the above

40) The CSS property which is used to define the set the difference between two lines of your content is -

A] min-height property

B] max-height property

C] line-height property

D] None of the above

41) Which of the following CSS property is used to add stroke to the text?

A] text-stroke property

B] text-transform property

C] text-decoration property

D] None of the above

42) Which of the following CSS property is used to set the blend mode for each background layer of an element?

A] background-blend-mode property

B] background-collapse property

C] background-transform property

D] background-origin property

43) The CSS property used to specify the transparency of an element is -

A] Hover

B] opacity

C] clearfix

D] overlay

44) Which of the following CSS property is used to set the horizontal alignment of a table-cell box or the block element?

A] text-align property

B] text-transform property

C] text-shadow property

D] text-decoration

45) The CSS property which is used to set the text wider or narrower compare to the default width of the font is -

A] font-stretch property

B] font-weight property

C] text-transform property

D] font-variant property

46) Which of the following CSS property is used to specify the type of quotation mark?

A] quotes property

B] z-index property

C] hyphens property

D] None of the above

47) The CSS property used to specify the order of flex item in the grid container is -

A] order property

B] float property

C] overflow property

D] None of the above

48) The CSS property used to set the indentation of the first line in a block of text is -

A] text-indent property

B] text-stroke property

C] text-decoration property

D] text-overflow property

49) Which of the following CSS property creates a clipping region and specifies the visible area of the element?

A] visibility property

B] background-clip property

C] clip-path property

D] None of the above

50) The correct syntax to give a line over text is -

A] text-decoration: line-through

B] text-decoration: none

C] text-decoration: overline

D] text-decoration: underline

1] Why so JavaScript and Java have similar name?

A] JavaScript is a stripped-down version of Java

B] JavaScript's syntax is loosely based on Java's

C] They both originated on the island of Java

D] None of the above

2] When a user views a page containing a JavaScript program, which machine actually executes the script?

A] The User's machine running a Web browser

B] The Web server

C] A central machine deep within Netscape's corporate offices

D] None of the above

3] ______ JavaScript is also called client-side JavaScript]

A] Microsoft

B] Navigator

C] LiveWire

D] Native

4] __________ JavaScript is also called server-side JavaScript]

A] Microsoft

B] Navigator

C] LiveWire

D] Native

5] What are variables used for in JavaScript Programs?

A] Storing numbers, dates, or other values

B] Varying randomly

C] Causing high-school algebra flashbacks

D] None of the above

6] _____ JavaScript statements embedded in an HTML page can respond to user events such as mouse-clicks, form input, and page navigation]

A] Client-side

B] Server-side

C] Local

D] Native

7] What should appear at the very end of your JavaScript?

The <script LANGUAGE="JavaScript">tag

A] The </script>

B] The <script>

C] The END statement

D] None of the above

8] Which of the following can't be done with client-side JavaScript?

A] Validating a form

B] Sending a form's contents by email

C] Storing the form's contents to a database file on the server

D] None of the above

9] Which of the following are capabilities of functions in JavaScript?

A] Return a value

B] Accept parameters and Return a value

C] Accept parameters

D] None of the above

10] Which of the following is not a valid JavaScript variable name?

A] 2names

B] _first_and_last_names

C] FirstAndLast

D] None of the above

11] _______ tag is an extension to HTML that can enclose any number of JavaScript statements]

A] <SCRIPT>

B] <BODY>

C] <HEAD>

D] <TITLE>

12] How does JavaScript store dates in a date object?

A] The number of milliseconds since January 1st, 1970

B] The number of days since January 1st, 1900

C] The number of seconds since Netscape's public stock offering]

D] None of the above

13] Which of the following attribute can hold the JavaScript version?

A] LANGUAGE

B] SCRIPT

C] VERSION

D] None of the above

14] What is the correct JavaScript syntax to write "Hello World"?

A] System]out]println("Hello World")

B] println ("Hello World")

C] document]write("Hello World")

D] response]write("Hello World")

15] Which of the following way can be used to indicate the LANGUAGE attribute?

A] <LANGUAGE="JavaScriptVersion">

B] <SCRIPT LANGUAGE="JavaScriptVersion">

C] <SCRIPT LANGUAGE="JavaScriptVersion"> JavaScript statements...</SCRIPT>

D] <SCRIPT LANGUAGE="JavaScriptVersion"!> JavaScript statements...</SCRIPT>

16] Inside which HTML element do we put the JavaScript?

A] <js>

B] <scripting>

C] <script>

D] <javascript>

17] What is the correct syntax for referring to an external script called " abc]js"?

A] <script href=" abc]js">

B] <script name=" abc]js">

C] <script src=" abc]js">

D] None of the above

18] Which types of image maps can be used with JavaScript?

A] Server-side image maps

B] Client-side image maps

C] Server-side image maps and Client-side image maps

D] None of the above

19] Which of the following navigator object properties is the same in both Netscape and IE?

A] navigator]appCodeName

B] navigator]appName

C] navigator]appVersion

D] None of the above

20] Which is the correct way to write a JavaScript array?

A] var txt = new Array(1:"tim",2:"kim",3:"jim")

B] var txt = new Array:1=("tim")2=("kim")3=("jim")

C] var txt = new Array("tim","kim","jim")

D] var txt = new Array="tim","kim","jim"

21] What does the <noscript> tag do?

A] Enclose text to be displayed by non-JavaScript browsers

B] Prevents scripts on the page from executing

C] Describes certain low-budget movies

D] None of the above

22] If para1 is the DOM object for a paragraph, what is the correct syntax to change the text within the paragraph?

A] "New Text"?

B] para1]value="New Text";

C] para1]firstChild]nodeValue= "New Text";

D] para1]nodeValue="New Text";

23] JavaScript entities start with _______ and end with _________

A] Semicolon, colon

B] Semicolon, Ampersand

C] Ampersand, colon

D] Ampersand, semicolon

24] Which of the following best describes JavaScript?

A] a low-level programming language

B] a scripting language precompiled in the browser

C] a compiled scripting language

D] an object-oriented scripting language

25] Choose the server-side JavaScript object?

A] FileUpLoad

B] Function

C] File

D] Date

26] Choose the client-side JavaScript object?

A] Database

B] Cursor

C] Client

D] File UpLoad

27] Which of the following is not considered a JavaScript operator?

A] new

B] this

C] delete

D] typeof

28] ______method evaluates a string of JavaScript code in the context of the specified object]

A] Eval
B] ParseInt
C] ParseFloat
D] Efloat

29] Which of the following event fires when the form element loses the focus: <button>, <input>, <label>, <select>, <textarea>?
A] onfocus
B] onblur
C] onclick
D] ondblclick

30] The syntax of Eval is ________________
A] [objectName]eval(numeric)
B] [objectName]eval(string)
C] [EvalName]eval(string)
D] [EvalName]eval(numeric)

31] JavaScript is interpreted by _________
A] Client
B] Server
C] Object
D] None of the above

32] Using _______ statement is how you test for a specific condition]
A] Select
B] If
C] Switch
D] For

33] Which of the following is the structure of an if statement?
A] if (conditional expression is true) thenexecute this codeend if
B] if (conditional expression is true)execute this codeend if
C] if (conditional expression is true) {then execute this code>->}
D] if (conditional expression is true) then {execute this code}

34] How to create a Date object in JavaScript?
A] dateObjectName = new Date([parameters])
B] dateObjectName.new Date([parameters])
C] dateObjectName := new Date([parameters])
D] dateObjectName Date([parameters])

35] The _______ method of an Array object adds and/or removes elements from an array]
A] Reverse

B] Shift

C] Slice

D] Splice

36] To set up the window to capture all Click events, we use which of the following statement?

A] window.captureEvents(Event.CLICK);

B] window.handleEvents (Event.CLICK);

C] window.routeEvents(Event.CLICK);

D] window.raiseEvents(Event.CLICK);

37] Which tag(s) can handle mouse events in Netscape?

A] <IMG>

B] <A>

C]

D] None of the above

38] ____________ is the tainted property of a window object

A] Pathname

B] Protocol

C] Defaultstatus

D] Host

39] To enable data tainting, the end user sets the _________ environment variable]

A] ENABLE_TAINT

B] MS_ENABLE_TAINT

C] NS_ENABLE_TAINT

D] ENABLE_TAINT_NS

40] In JavaScript, _________ is an object of the target language data type that encloses an object of the source language]

A] a wrapper

B] a link

C] a cursor

D] a form

41] When a JavaScript object is sent to Java, the runtime engine creates a Java wrapper of type ___________

A] ScriptObject

B] JSObject

C] JavaObject

D] Jobject

42] ________ class provides an interface for invoking JavaScript methods and examining JavaScript properties]

A] ScriptObject

B] JSObject

C] JavaObject

D] Jobject

43] __________ is a wrapped Java array, accessed from within JavaScript code]

A] JavaArray

B] JavaClass

C] JavaObject

D] JavaPackage

44] A ________ object is a reference to one of the classes in a Java package, such as netscape]javascript]

A] JavaArray

B] JavaClass

C] JavaObject

D] JavaPackage

45] The JavaScript exception is available to the Java code as an instance of ___________

A] netscape.javascript.JSObject

B] netscape.javascript.JSException

C] netscape.plugin.JSException

D] None of the above

46] To automatically open the console when a JavaScript error occurs which of the following is added to prefs]js?

A] user_pref(" javascript]console]open_on_error", false);

B] user_pref("javascript.console]open_error ", true);

C] user_pref("javascript.console]open_error ", false);

D] user_pref("javascript.console]open_on_error", true);

47] To open a dialog box each time an error occurs, which of the following is added to prefs]js?

A] user_pref("javascript]classic.error_alerts", true);

B] user_pref("javascript]classic.error_alerts ", false);

C] user_pref("javascript]console.open_on_error ", true);

D] user_pref("javascript]console.open_on_error ", false);

48] The syntax of a blur method in a button object is _______________

A] Blur()

B] Blur(contrast)

C] Blur(value)

D] Blur(depth)

49] The syntax of capture events method for document object is ______________

A] captureEvents()

B] captureEvents(args eventType)

C] captureEvents(eventType)

D] captureEvents(eventVal)

50] The syntax of close method for document object is ______________

A] Close(doC]

B] Close(object)

C] Close(val)

D] Close()

1] The programming environment which permits coding, compilation, running and debugging from a single window is called

(a) Integrated Development Environment (IDE)

(b) Editor

(c) Highlighter

(d) Compiler

2] The IDE of VBA supports since it permits drag and drop approach for design of user interface

(a) Procedural Approach

(b) reverse approach

(c) Rapid Application Development (RAD)

(d) postfix approach

3] VBA permits of data from spreadsheets

(a) reading

(b) writing

(c) both reading and writing

(d) neither reading nor writing

4] VBA supports ready made user interface components like

(a) UserForm, CommandButton

(b) Label, TextBox, ComboBox, ListBox

(c) TabStrip, OptionButton, ToggleButton

(d) all of them

5] VBA supports through class module

(a) Object Oriented Programming System (OOPS)

(b) Procedural programming
(c) Functional programming
(d) property based model
6] VBA can be used to automate carried out through MS Excel
(a) data processing
(b) graphing
(c) accessing cell values
(d) <u>all of them</u>
7] VBA code is compiled into an intermediate code called code
(a) <u>P-Code</u>
(b) MicroSoft Intermediate Code (MSIL)
(c) Java Virtual Machine (JVM) code
(d) Android Virtual Device (AVD) code
8] MS Excel creates to execute VBA code
(a) real time computer
(b) mobile computer
(c) tablet computer
(d) <u>virual machine</u>
9] ____is the shortcut to open VBA IDE from MS Excel
(a) <u>Alt+F11</u>
(b) Alt+F8
(c) Ctrl+Break
(d) Ctrl+G
10]________ is the shortcut to open immediate window in VBA IDE
(a) Alt+F11
(b) Alt+F8
(c) Ctrl+Break
(d) <u>Ctrl+G</u>
11] ________is the shortcut to open list of macros
(a) Alt+F11
(b) <u>Alt+F8</u>
(c) Ctrl+ Break
(d) Ctrl+ G
12] is the shortcut to stop execution of programs in VBA IDE
(a) Alt+F11
(b) Alt+F8
(c) <u>Ctrl+ Break</u>
(d) Ctrl+ G

13] ______ is the shortcut to display information relating to selected component in VBA IDE

(a) Ctrl+I
(b) Ctrl+J
(c) Ctrl+R
(d) Ctrl+Shift+I

14] ______is the shortcut to properties and methods of a component in VBA IDE

(a) Ctrl+ I
(b) Ctrl+ J
(c) Ctrl+ R
(d) Ctrl+ Shift+ I

15]______ is the shortcut to display project explorer in VBA IDE

(a) Ctrl+ I
(b) Ctrl+ J
(c) Ctrl+ R
(d) Ctrl+ Shift+ I

16] ______is the shortcut to display parameter information for selected element in VBA IDE

(a) Ctrl +I
(b) Ctrl+ J
(c) Ctrl+ R
(d) Ctrl+ Shift+ I

17] ______is the shortcut to add breakpoint in VBA IDE

(a) F9
(b) F5
(c) F1
(d) F2

18] ______is the shortcut to display object browser in VBA IDE

(a) F9
(b) F5
(c) F1
(d) F2

19] ______is the shortcut to display properties window in VBA IDE

(a) F4
(b) F5
(c) F1
(d) F2

20]__________structure is useful for decision involving three or more options

a) Switch

b) Select case

c) Function

d) List

21] VBA has a coding, compilation, running and debugging environment called

(a) Integrated Development Environment (IDE)

(b) Editor

(c) Highlighter

(d) Compiler

22] In VBA, the function Asc converts given character value to numeric code in______ system

(a) American Standard Code for Information Interchange (ASCII)

(b) Double Byte Character Set (DBCS)

(c) Unicode

(d) none of them

23] In VBA, the function AscB converts given character value to numeric code in ______system]

(a) American Standard Code for Information Interchange (ASCII)

(b) Double Byte Character Set (DBCS)

(c) Unicode

(d) none of them

24] In VBA, the function AscW converts given character value to numeric code in ________system

(a) American Standard Code for Information Interchange (ASCII)

(b) Double Byte Character Set (DBCS)

(c) Unicode

(d) none of them

25] In VBA, the function Chr converts given numeric value to character value in _______system

(a) American Standard Code for Information Interchange (ASCII)

(b) Double Byte Character Set (DBCS)

(c) Unicode

(d) none of them

26] In VBA, the function ChrB converts given numeric value to character value in ______system]

(a) American Standard Code for Information Interchange (ASCII)
(b) Double Byte Character Set (DBCS)
(c) Unicode
(d) none of them

27] In VBA, the function ChrW converts given numeric value to character value in ________system
(a) American Standard Code for Information Interchange (ASCII)
(b) Double Byte Character Set (DBCS)
(c) Unicode System
(d) none of them

28] In VBA, Cstr function converts any data to______ type
(a) Integer
(b) Double
(c) Single
(d) String

29] CDbl function converts String to __________type
(a) Integer
(b) Double
(c) Single
(d) String

30] In VBA, CInt function converts String to ________type
(a) Integer
(b) Double
(c) Single
(d) String

31] In VBA, Csng function converts String to ________type]
(a) Integer
(b) Double
(c) Single
(d) String

32] In VBA, Val function converts String to ________type
(a) number
(b) byte
(c) Currency
(d) Decimal

33] In VBA, CByte function converts String to _______type
(a) number
(b) byte

(c) Currency
(d) Decimal
34] In VBA, CCur function converts String to ________type
(a) number
(b) byte
(c) Currency
(d) Decimal
35] In VBA, CLng function converts String to________ type
(a) Long
(b) byte
(c) Currency
(d) Decimal
36] In VBA, CDec function converts String to________ type
(a) number
(b) byte
(c) Currency
(d) Decimal
37] _______function in VBA creates a custom error message
(a) Format
(b) CVErr
(c) InputBox
(d) MsgBox
38] _________function in VBA formats a number according to given text strings containing 0, # and comma (,)
(a) Format
(b) CVErr
(c) InputBox
(d) MsgBox
39] Boolean data type in VBA has size of _______
(a) 1 byte
(b) 2 bytes
(c) 3 bytes
(d) 4 bytes
40] Byte data type in VBA has size of_________
(a) 1 byte
(b) 2 bytes
(c) 3 bytes
(d) 4 bytes

1] Company restore option is available in ________

a) Company reset

b) New company

c) company information

d) Edit company

2] To change current Date from Gateway of tally press the key ____

a) F1

b) F2

c) F3

d) F4

3] Tally supports ________ system of accounting

(a) single entry

(b) double entry

(c) no entry

(d) null entry

4] Tally can maintain ________ for stock keeping, so that fresh inventory may arrive before the old stock is exhausted

(a) reorder level

(b) profit

(c) loss

(d) cash

5] Balance sheet is produced ________when accounts are maintained in Tally

(a) manually

(b) automatically

(c) remotely

(d) randomly

6] The statement of account debits, credits, assets and liabilities is called______

(a) stock& inventory report

(b) profit & loss account

(c) balance sheet

(d) cash balance

7] Pressing _______button in the Gateway of Tally opens company info in Tally

(a) Alt+F3

(b) F11

(c) F5

(d) F6

8] Pressing______ key opens accounting features

(a) Alt+F3

(b) F11

(c) F5

(d) F6

9] Payroll, budgeting and scenario management may be enabled through ______menu in Tally

(a) Accounting Features

(b) Inventory Features

(c) Statutory and Taxation

(d) none of them

10] Account Groups, Ledgers, Budget and scenario are available under ______ in Tally

(a) Payroll Info

(b) Inventory Info

(c) Accounts Info

(d) none of them

11] Inventory groups, (categories, if needed), items, units of measure, reorder level, inventory vouchers, etc are available under _______in Tally

(a) Payroll Info

(b) Inventory Info

(c) Accounts Info

(d) none of them

12] Employee groups, employee, attendance/production types, pay heads,salary details, voucher types, etc. areavailable under in Tally

(a) Payroll Info

(b) Inventory Info

(c) Accounts Info

(d) none of them

13]_____ is the shortcut to create contra voucher in Tally

(a) F6

(b) F5

(c) F4

(d) F2

14]______ is the shortcut to create payment voucher in Tally

(a) F6

(b) F5

(c) F4
(d) F2
15] ______ is the shortcut to create receipt voucher in Tally
(a) <u>F6</u>
(b) F5
(c) F4
(d) F2
16] ______ is the shortcut to configure a company in Tally
(a) F6
(b) F5
(c) F4
(d) <u>F12</u>
17] ______ is the shortcut to change the accounting period from Gateway of Tally
(a) F1
(b) Alt+F1
(c) <u>Alt+F2</u>
(d) Alt+F3
18] ______ is the shortcut to shut a company in Tally
(a) F1
(b) <u>Alt+F1</u>
(c) Alt+F2
(d) Alt+F3
19] ______ is the shortcut to company info from Gateway of Tally
(a) F1
(b) Alt+F1
(c) Alt+F2
(d) <u>Alt+F3</u>
20] ______is the shortcut to inventory buttons from Accounting Vouchers in Tally
(a) <u>Alt+F1</u>
(b) Ctrl+F1
(c) F7
(d) F8
21]______ is the shortcut to payroll buttons from Accounting Vouchers in Tally
(a) Alt+F1
(b) <u>Ctrl+F1</u>

(c) F7
(d) F8

22] _____ is the shortcut to Journal from Accounting Vouchers in Tally
(a) Alt+F1
(b) Ctrl+F1
(c) F7
(d) F8

23] _____is the shortcut to sales voucher from Accounting Vouchers in Tally
(a) Alt+F1
(b) Ctrl+F1
(c) F9
(d) F8

24] ______ is the shortcut to purchase voucher from Accounting Vouchers in Tally
(a) Alt+F1
(b) Ctrl+F1
(c) F9
(d) F8

25] ______is the shortcut to credit note from Accounting Vouchers in Tally
(a) Alt+F1
(b) Ctrl+F1
(c) Ctrl+F9
(d) Ctrl+F8

26] _____ is the shortcut to debit note from Accounting Vouchers in Tally]
(a) Alt+F1
(b) Ctrl+F1
(c) Ctrl+F9
(d) Ctrl+F8

27]______ is the shortcut to reversing journal from Accounting Vouchers in Tally
(a) F10
(b) Ctrl+F10
(c) Alt+I
(d) Alt+V

28]______is the shortcut to reversing journal from Accounting Vouchers in Tally

(a) F10

(b) Ctrl+F10

(c) Alt+I

(d) Alt+V

29] _____ is the shortcut to Memos from Accounting Vouchers in Tally

(a) F10

(b) Ctrl+F10

(c) Alt+I

(d) Alt+V

30] _____ is the shortcut to Accounting Invoice from Accounting Vouchers in Tally

(a) F10

(b) Ctrl+F10

(c) Alt +I

(d) Alt +V

31] ______ is the shortcut to voucher as invoice from Accounting Vouchers in Tally

(a) F10

(b) Ctrl+F10

(c) Alt +I

(d) Ctrl +V

32]______ is the shortcut to postdated voucher from Accounting Vouchers in Tally

(a) Ctrl+ T

(b) Ctrl+F10

(c) Alt +I

(d) Ctrl +V

33]______ is the shortcut to optional voucher from Accounting Vouchers in Tally

(a) Ctrl +T

(b) Ctrl +L

(c) Alt +I

(d) Ctrl +V

34]______ is the shortcut to Payroll from Payroll Vouchers in Tally

(a) Alt+ A

(b) Alt+ S

(c) Ctrl+ F5
(d) Alt+F4

35] ______ is the shortcut to Attendance from Payroll Vouchers in Tally
(a) Alt+ A
(b) Alt+ S
(c) Ctrl+F5
(d) Ctrl+F4

36] ______ is the shortcut to Payroll as Voucher from Payroll Vouchers in Tally
(a) Alt+ A
(b) Alt+ S
(c) Ctrl+F5
(d) Ctrl+F4

37] ______ is the shortcut to Payroll Auto fill from Payroll Vouchers in Tally
(a) Alt+ A
(b) Alt+ S (c) Ctrl+F5
(d) Ctrl+F4

38] ______ is the shortcut to purchase order from Payroll Vouchers in Tally
(a) Alt+F4
(b) Alt+F5
(c) Ctrl+F5
(d) Ctrl+F4

39] ______ is the shortcut to sales order from Payroll Vouchers in Tally
(a) Alt+F4
(b) Alt+F5
(c) Ctrl+F5
(d) Ctrl+F4

40] ______ is the shortcut to physical stock verification from Inventory Vouchers in Tally
(a) Alt+F4
(b) Alt+F5
(c) Alt+F7
(d) Alt+F10

41] ______ is the shortcut to stock journal from Inventory Vouchers in Tally
(a) Alt+F4

(b) Alt+F5

(c) Alt+F7

(d) Alt+F10

42]_____ is the shortcut to rejection in from Inventory Vouchers in Tally

(a) Alt+F6

(b) Ctrl+F6

(c) Alt+F8

(d) Alt+F9

43]______ is the shortcut to rejection out from Inventory Vouchers in Tally

(a) Alt+F6

(b) Ctrl+F6

(c) Alt+F8

(d) Alt+F9

44] _____ is the shortcut to Indent from Inventory Vouchers in Tally

(a) Alt+F6

(b) Ctrl+F7

(c) Alt+F8

(d) Alt+F9

45] _____ is the shortcut to delivery note from Inventory Vouchers in Tally

(a) Alt+F6

(b) Ctrl+F7

(c) Alt+F8

(d) Alt+F9

46] ______ is the shortcut to receipt note from Inventory Vouchers in Tally

(a) Alt+F6

(b) Ctrl+F7

(c) Alt+F8

(d) Alt+F9

47] Tally maintains account using _______ entry system of accounting

(a) single

(b) double

(c) triple

(d) quadruple

48] Entering each transaction in debit and credit columns is called____ entry system of accounting

(a) single

(b) double

(c) triple

(d) quadruple

49] Prior allocation of money for specific purposes using Tally is called_____

(a) budgeting

(b) scenario

(c) inventory

(d) voucher entry

50] Progress of expenses against budget allocation may be compared to the trial balance of original company using _______menu in Trial Balance

(a) Budget (Alt+ B)

(b) Column (Alt+ C)

(c) F6

(d) F7

Ans] a

1] Which of the following describes e-commerce?

A] doing business electronically

B] doing business

C] sale of goods

D] all of the above

2] Which of the following is part of the four main types for e-commerce?

A] b2b

B] b2c

C] c2b

D] all of the above

3] Which segment do eBay, Amazon]com belong?

A] b2bs

B] b2cs

C] c2bs

D] c2cs

4] Which type of e-commerce focuses on consumers dealing with each other?

A] b2b

B] b2c

C] c2b

D] c2c

5] Which segment is eBay an example?

A] b2b

B] c2b

C] c2c

D] none of the above

6] Which type deals with auction?

A] b2b

B] b2c

C] c2b

D] c2c

7] In which website Global Easy Buy is facilitated?

A] ebay.com

B] amazon.com

C] yepme.com

D] none of these

8] The best products to sell in B2C e-commerce are:

A] small products

B] digital products

C] specialty products

D] fresh products

9] Which products are people most likely to be more uncomfortable buying on the Internet?

A] books

B] furniture

C] movies

D] all of the above

10] Which products are people most likely to be comfortable buying on the Internet?

A] books

B] pcs

C] cds

D] all of the above

11] Digital products are best suited for B2C e-commerce because they:

A] are commodity like products

B] can be mass-customized and personalized

C] can be delivered at the time of purchase

D] all of the above

12] The solution for all business needs is

A] edi

B] erp

C] scm

D] none of the above

13] All of the following are techniques B2C e-commerce companies use to attract customers, except:

A] registering with search engines

B] viral marketing

C] online ads

D] virtual marketing

14] Which is a function of E-commerce

A] marketing

B] advertising

C] warehousing

D] all of the above

15] Which is not a function of E-commerce

A] marketing

B] advertising

C] warehousing

D] none of the above

16] Which term represents a count of the number of people who visit one site, click on an ad, and are taken to the site of the advertiser?

A] affiliate programs

B] click-through

C] spam

D] all of the above

17] What is the percentage of customers who visit a Web site and actually buy something called?

A] affiliate programs

B] click-through

C] spam

D] conversion rate

18] What are materials used in production in a manufacturing company or are placed on the shelf for sale in a retail environment?

A] direct materials

B] indirect materials

C] edi

D] none of the above

19] What are materials that are necessary for running a modern corporation, but do not relate to the company's primary business activities?

A] direct materials

B] <u>indirect materials</u>

C] edi

D] none of the above

20] What are ballpoint pens purchased by a clothing company?

A] direct materials

B] <u>indirect materials</u>

C] edi

D] none of the above

21] What is another name for?

A] direct materials

B] <u>indirect materials</u>

C] edi

D] none of the above

22] What is the process in which a buyer posts its interest in buying a certain quantity of items, and sellers compete for the business by submitting successively lower bids until there is only one seller left?

A] b2b marketplace

B] intranet

C] <u>reverse auction</u>

D] internet

23] What are plastic cards the size of a credit card that contains an embedded chip on which digital information can be stored?

A] customer relationship management systems cards

B] e-government identity cards

C] fedi cards

D] <u>smart cards</u>

24] Most individuals are familiar with which form of e-commerce?

A] b2b

B] <u>b2c</u>

C] c2b

D] c2c

25] Which form of e-commerce currently accounts for about 97% of all e-commerce revenues?

A] b2b
B] b2c
C] c2b
D] c2c

26] Which of the following are advantages normally associated with B2B e-commerce?

A] shorter cycle times
B] reduction in costs
C] reaches wider audiences
D] all of the above

27] If the threat of substitute products or services is low it is a(n):

A] disadvantage to the supplier
B] advantage to the buyer
C] advantage to the supplier
D] none of the above

28] The threat of new entrants is high when it is:

A] hard for customers to enter the market
B] hard for competitors to enter the market
C] easy for competitors to enter the market
D] easy for customers to enter the market

29] If it is easy for competitors to enter the market, the threat of new entrants is considered:

A] high
B] low
C] more
D] less

30] An industry is less attractive for suppliers when the rivalry among existing competitors is:

A] high
B] low
C] more
D] less

31] Unique value auction is mainly applies to?

A] new products
B] second hand products
C] engineering products
D] none of the above

32] Paisapay is facilitated in

A] ebay]co.in

B] amazon.com

C] flipkart.com

D] none of the above

33] Which of the following is a useful security mechanism when considering business strategy and IT?

A] encryption

B] decryption

C] firewall

D] all the above

34] Which of the following is not related to security mechanism

A] encryption

B] decryption

C] e-cash

D] all the above

35] A product or service that customers have come to expect from an industry, which must be offered by new entrants if they wish to compete and survive, is known as a(n)?

A] switching costs

B] loyalty programs

C] entry barriers

D] affiliate programs

36] Which of the following statements accurately reflect the impact of technology?

A] technology has caused buyer power to increase

B] technology has lessened the entry barriers for many industrie

C] technology has increased the threat of substitute products and services

D] all of the above

37] A business cannot be all things to all people] Instead, a business must:

A] identify target customers

B] identify the value of products/services as perceived by customers

C] all of the above

D] none of the above

38] How the transactions occur in e-commerce?

A] using e-medias

B] using computers only

C] using mobile phones only

D] none of the above

39] Which type of products is lesser purchased using ecommerce?

A] automobiles

B] books

C] softwares

D] none

40] A business competing in a commodity like environment must focus on which of the following?

A] price

B] ease / speed of delivery

C] ease of ordering

D] all of the above

41] Which of the following refers to creating products tailored to individual customers?

A] customization

B] aggregation

C] direct materials

D] reverse auction

42] Materials used in the normal operation of a business but not related to primary business operations are called what?

A] supplies

B] direct materials

C] indirect materials

D] daily stuff

43] Amazon]com is well-known for which e-commerce marketing technique?

A] banner ads

B] pop-up ads

C] affiliate programs

D] viral marketing

44] What is the name given to an interactive business providing a centralized market where many buyers and suppliers can come together for e-commerce or commerce-related activities?

A] direct marketplace

B] b2b

C] b2c

D] electronic marketplace

45] Which form of e-marketplace brings together buyers and sellers from multiple industries, often for MRO materials?

A] horizontal

B] vertical

C] integrated

D] inclined

46] Which form of e-marketplace brings together buyers and sellers from the same industry?

A] horizontal

B] vertical

C] integrated

D] inclined

47] Which type of add appears on a web page?

A] pop-under ad

B] pop-up ad

C] banner ad

D] discount ad

48] What type of ad appears on top of a web page?

A] pop-under ad

B] pop-up ad

C] banner ad

D] discount ad

49] What type of ad appears under a web page?

A] pop-under ad

B] pop-up ad

C] banner ad

D] discount ad

50] Which, if any, of the following types of ads are people most willing to tolerate?

A] pop-under ad

B] pop-up ad

C] banner ad

D] none of the above

Q. 1 ________ is the practice and precautions taken to protect valuable information from unauthorized access, recording, disclosure or destruction.

A] Network Security

B] Database Security

C] Information Security

D] Physical Security

Q. 2 ________ platforms are used for safety and protection of information in the cloud.

A] Cloud workload protection platforms

B] Cloud security protocols

C] AWS

D] One Drive

Q. 3 Compromising confidential information comes under__

A] Bug

B] Threat

C] Vulnerability

D] Attack

Q. 4 An attempt to harm, damage or cause threat to a system or network is broadly termed as _______

A] Cyber-crime

B] Cyber Attack

C] System hijacking

D] Digital crime

Q. 5 The CIA triad is often represented by which of the following?

A] Triangle

B] Diagonal

C] Ellipse

D] Circle

Q. 6 Related to information security, confidentiality is the opposite of which of the following?

A] Closure

B] Disclosure

C] Disaster

D] Disposal

Q. 8 ________ means the protection of data from modification by unknown users.

A] Confidentiality

B] Integrity

C] Authentication

D] Non-repudiation

Q. 9 ________ of information means, only authorized users are capable of accessing the information.

A] Confidentiality

B] Integrity

C] Non-repudiation

D] Availability

Q. 10 This helps in identifying the origin of information and authentic user. This referred to here as __________

A] Confidentiality

B] Integrity

C] Authenticity

D] Availability

Q. 11 Data ___________ is used to ensure confidentiality.

A] Encryption

B] Locking

C] Decryption

D] Backup

Q. 12 What does OSI stand for in the OSI Security Architecture?

A] Open System Interface

B] Open Systems Interconnections

C] Open Source Initiative

D] Open Standard Interconnections

Q. 13 A company requires its users to change passwords every month. This improves the ________ of the network.

A] Performance

B] Reliability

C] Security

D] None of the above

Q. 14 Release of message contents and Traffic analysis are two types of _________ attacks.

A] Active Attack

B] Modification of Attack

C] Passive attack

D] DoS Attack

Q. 15 The ________ is encrypted text.

A] Cipher scricpt

B] Cipher text

C] Secret text

D] Secret script

Q. 17 Which of the following Algorithms not belong to symmetric encryption

A] 3DES (TripleDES)

B] RSA

C] RC5

D] IDEA

Q. 18 Which is the largest disadvantage of the symmetric Encryption?

A] More complex and therefore more time-consuming calculations.

B] Problem of the secure transmission of the Secret Key.

C] Less secure encryption function.

D] Isn't used any more.

Q. 19 In cryptography, what is cipher?

A] algorithm for performing encryption and decryption

B] encrypted message

C] both algorithm for performing encryption and decryption and encrypted message

D] decrypted message

Q. 21 Which one of the following algorithm is not used in asymmetric-key cryptography?

A] rsa algorithm

B] diffie-hellman algorithm

C] electronic code book algorithm

D] dsa algorithm

Q. 23 What is data encryption standard (DES)?

A] block cipher

B] stream cipher

C] bit cipher

D] byte cipher

Q. 24 A asymmetric-key (or public key) cipher uses

A] 1 key

B] 2 key

C] 3 key

D] 4 key

Q. 26 ________________ is the process or mechanism used for converting ordinary plain text into garbled non-human readable text & vice-versa.

A] Malware Analysis

B] Exploit writing

C] Reverse engineering

D] Cryptography

Q.27 ______________ is a means of storing & transmitting information in a specific format so that only those for whom it is planned can understand or process it.

A] Malware Analysis

B] <u>Cryptography</u>

C] Reverse engineering

D] Exploit writing

Q. 28 Cryptographic algorithms are based on mathematical algorithms where these algorithms use ___________ for a secure transformation of data.

A] <u>secret key</u>

B] external programs

C] add-ons

D] secondary key

Q. 29 Conventional cryptography is also known as _____________ or symmetric-key encryption.

A] <u>secret-key</u>

B] public key

C] protected key

D] primary key

Q. 30 The procedure to add bits to the last block is termed as _________________

A] decryption

B] hashing

C] tuning

D] <u>padding</u>

Q. 32 ECC encryption system is __________

A] symmetric key encryption algorithm

B] <u>asymmetric key encryption algorithm</u>

C] not an encryption algorithm

D] block cipher method

Q. 33 ________function creates a message digest out of a message.

A] encryption

B] decryption

C] <u>hash</u>

D] none of the above

Q. 34 Extensions to the X.509 certificates were added in version ____

A] 1

B] 2

C] 3

D] 4

Q. 35 A digital signature needs _____ system

A] symmetric-key

B] asymmetric-key

C] either (a) or (b)

D] neither (a) nor (b)

Q. 36 Elliptic curve cryptography follows the associative property.

A] TRUE

B] FALSE

Q. 37 ECC stands for

A] Elliptic curve cryptography

B] Enhanced curve cryptography

C] Elliptic cone cryptography

D] Eclipse curve cryptography

Q. 38 When a hash function is used to provide message authentication, the hash function value is referred to as

A] Message Field

B] Message Digest

C] Message Score

D] Message Leap

Q. 39 Message authentication code is also known as

A] key code

B] hash code

C] keyed hash function

Q. 40 The main difference in MACs and digital signatures is that, in digital signatures the hash value of the message is encrypted with a user's public key.

A] TRUE

B] FALSE

Q. 41 The DSS signature uses which hash algorithm?

A] MD5

B] SHA-2

C] SHA-1

D] Does not use hash algorithm

Q. 42 What is the size of the RSA signature hash after the MD5 and SHA-1 processing?

A] 42 bytes

B] 32 bytes

C] 36 bytes

D] 48 bytes

Q. 43 In the handshake protocol which is the message type first sent between client and server ?

A] server_hello

B] client_hello

C] hello_request

D] certificate_request

Q. 44 One commonly used public-key cryptography method is the ______ algorithm.

A] RSS

B] RAS

C] RSA

D] RAA

Q. 45 The ________ method provides a one-time session key for two parties.

A] Diffie-Hellman

B] RSA

C] DES

D] AES

Q. 46 The _________ attack can endanger the security of the Diffie-Hellman method if two parties are not authenticated to each other.

A] man-in-the-middle

B] ciphertext attack

C] plaintext attack

D] none of the above

Q. 48 VPN is abbreviated as __________

A] Visual Private Network

B] Virtual Protocol Network

C] Virtual Private Network

D] Virtual Protocol Networking

Q. 49 __________ provides an isolated tunnel across a public network for sending and receiving data privately as if the computing devices were directly connected to the private network.

A] Visual Private Network

B] Virtual Protocol Network

C] Virtual Protocol Networking

D] Virtual Private Network

Q. 50 Which of the statements are not true to classify VPN systems?

A] Protocols used for tunnelling the traffic

B] Whether VPNs are providing site-to-site or remote access connection

C] Securing the network from bots and malwares

D] Levels of security provided for sending and receiving data privately

INDUSTRIAL TRAINING INSTITUTE

Monthly Test-1, Marks- 20, Date:- _______________

(Every Question Carry Two Marks)

1] ABC stands for --------------

A] Automatic Breathing Control

B] Automatic Blood Control

C] Airway Breathing Circulation

D] Automatic Blood Circulation

3] To put off"Class B" fire, the types of fire extinguisher used is ....

A] dry power

B] Carbon dioxide

C] Jet of water

D] Foam type

4] Which type of fire extinguisher is used to put off general fire?

A] Water type Extinguisher

B] Foam type Extinguisher

C] Dry chemical powder Extinguisher

D] Carbon dioxide (C02] Extinguisher

5] In case of bleeding, take treatment Of

D] cold 3" and rest

A] spray cold water

B] Bandage immediately -----.

B] Enquire about the accident thought treatment

6] in case of an accident, the victim should im

A] Asked to take rest

C] Attended immediately

D] leave him

7] First aid is given to an injured or ill person primarily....

A] Save life

B] Prevent further deterioration of the muff's

C] Give best possible comfort

D] All of these

Q.1. Which of the following is the biggest unit of memory?

A] Gigabytes.

B] bytes.

C] Megabytes.

D] Kilobytes.

Q.2. The primary purpose of software is to turn data into.

A] Website.

B] Infromation.

C] Programs.

D] Objects.

Q.3. GUI Stands for

A] Graphical User Interface.

B] Greater User Interface.

C] Graphical Union Interface.

D] Graphical User Intereat.

Q.4. Key board keys that have arrows on them are called -

A] Function Keys.

B] Navigation Keys.

C] Typewriter Keys.

D] Special purpose keys.

INDUSTRIAL TRAINING INSTITUTE

Monthly Test-2, Marks- 20, Date:- _______________

(Every Question Carry Two Marks)

Q.12. .... can be used to create and format large and complex text documents.

A] "Calculator"

B] "WordPad"

C] "Notepad"

D] "Text Pad"

Q.14. A folder system is also called a "................"

A] "Direction System"

B] "Directory System"

C] "Directory list"

D] "Folder book"

Q.17. A .... is like a container in which you can store files.

A] "Icon"

B] "document"

C] "Folder"

D] "Sheet"

Q.18. The operating system's job is .... to

A] Execute many useful commands easily.

B] to make request for service through a defined application programme interface.

C] to control the computer at the most fundamental level.

D] None of these.

Q.19. The windows interface is based on ....

A] "Graphical user Interface" or GUI

B] Application Programme Interface or] API.

C] "Clipboard"

D] None of these

Q.23. A file created using Notepad is stored with the extension.................. .

A] ".txt"

B] ".docx"

C] ".png"

D] ".jpg"

Q.25. When your computer is booted and is ready to use, the screen you see is called the ....

A] "Table top"

B] "Desktop"

C] "Laptop"

D] None of these

Q.27. .... is designed to prevent and remove spy ware.

A] User Account Control

B] Windows Firewall

C] Windows Defender

D] Parental Controls

Q.29. What is "Windows Aero"

A] It is the graphical user interface for Windows XP.

B] It is the graphical user interface for Windows Vista.

C] Application Program

D] None of these

Q.30. Which is the basic program of a computer?

A] Operating System

B] Software Program

C] Application Program

D] None of these

INDUSTRIAL TRAINING INSTITUTE

Monthly Test-3, Marks- 20, Date:- ______________

(Every Question Carry Two Marks)

Q.34. The .... Menu is used to enhance the appearance of the contained presented in a document.

A] "Insert"

B] "Edit" ?

C] "Format"

D] "File"

Q.36. "............." helps in guarding your computer against malicious software.

A] "Windows Firewall"

B] "Windows Defender"

C] "Spy ware"

D] of these.

Q.37. .... is a basic text editing programme and it is most commonly used to view or edit text files.

A] "Calculator"

B] "Notepad"

C] "Address book"

D] "Paint"

Q.38. In a windows operating system screen saver

A] is helps in guarding your computer against many types of malicious software.

B] is a long, vertical bar that is displayed on the side of your desktop.

C] is a programme that displays on image, animation, or just a blank screen on a Computer after on input has been received for a certain length of time.

D] None of these.

Q.40. The programmes on the .... in Windows Vista remain there and are always available for you to click to start them.

A] the "Most frequently use programmes list.

B] "pinned items list"

C] "Documents"

D] "Control Panel"

Q.41. In Windows Vista .... is a power-saving state.

A] Log off

B] Sleep

C] Restart

D] Lock

Q.42. AERO is an abbreviation of ....

A] Authentic, Energetic, Reflective and Open.

B] Essential, Reflective and Open.

C] Arithmetic, Essential, Reflective and Object.

D] Authentic, Essential, Reflective and Open.

Q.43. At the bottom of the screen, you can see a long, thin bar which is called as ....

A] "Task bar"

B] "Title bar"

C] "Mcnu bar"

D] "Spacebar"

Q.44. In Windows Vista a "Clipboard" is ....

A] an application program

B] a temporary storage area for information that you have copied or moved from one place and plan to use somewhere else.

C] an operating system.

D] None of these.

Q.45. .... is a basic text editing programme and it is most commonly used to view or edit text files.

A] "Calculator"

B] "Notepad"

C] "Address book"

D] "Paint"

INDUSTRIAL TRAINING INSTITUTE

Monthly Test-4, Marks- 20, Date:- _______________

(Every Question Carry Two Marks)

Q.46. ...., is a drawing programme that can be used to create modify graphic images.

A] "Brush"

B] "Paint"

C] "Notepad"

D] "WordPad"

Q.5. All of the following Ribbon tabs are displayed in Word 2007, EXCEPT

A] Home

B] Insert

C] Tools

D] Page Layout

Q.9. In Word, a file is called as a ....

A] "template"

B] "form"

C] "database"

D] "Document"

Q.13. A .... is a reference from one part of a document to related information in same another part.

A] Hyperlink

B] Cross-reference

C] Document

D] Linkage

Q.14. For Indentation you may use the "Decrease Indent" and "Increase Indent" icons in the "Paragraph" group on the "............" tab for indenting your text.

A] Insert

B] Home

C] Page Layout

D] Data

Q.16. The "..............." is a dictionary of synonyms which you can use to find words that are synonyms with a term.

A] Translate

B] Spelling

C] Thesaurus

D] Research

Q.17. A " .... " is a listing of the topics that appear in a document with their associated page references.

A] Index

B] Table

C] Clipboard

D] Table of contents

Q.19. A "............." is a connection to a location in the current document to another document or Web Site.

A] Link

B] hyperlink

C] hypolink

D] linkage

Q.26. A "................" is a pre-designed document useful for creating common purpose documents such as a fax, invoice or business letter.

A] Template

B] File

C] Form

D] Database

Q.28. A "............" is used to organize information into an easy-to-read format of horizontal rows and vertical columns.

A] Cell

B] Sheet

C] Box

D] Table

INDUSTRIAL TRAINING INSTITUTE

Monthly Test-5, Marks- 20, Date:- ______________

(Every Question Carry Two Marks)

Q.29. To remove individual character at the left you may press "............".

A] Delete

B] Backspace

C] Enter

D] Spacebar

Q.30. When you click on "Format Printer" icon on the "Home" tab, you can see that your mouse pointer changes to a "............" icon.

A] paintbrush

B] I-beam

C] Arrow

D] 4-Way arrow

Q.33. When you move your mouse over a button, a .... is displayed. That provides a detailed description of what the button does.

A] Super-tooltip

B] Sub-tooltip

C] Info

D] Key-tip

Q.35. .... Applications help you to create different types of written documents such as personal letters, from letters, brochures, faxes and even professional manuals.

A] Word Processor

B] Word Pad

C] Note Pad

D] None of these

Q.40. To automatically correct the document, we use

A] The auto correct feature

B] The auto complete feature

C] Formatting

D] Building Blocks

Q.41. A "..............." is a common application for news paper columns.

A] News reading

B] News letter

C] News

D] News editor

Q.47. A "............." is used to mark a certain location in a document.

A] Index

B] Hyperlink

C] Bookmark

D] Table

Q.50. While changing the level of an item in hierarchy you can increase the indent by using

A] "Tab"

B] "Backspace"

C] "Delete"

D] "Spacebar"

Q.51. Footnotes or Endnotes are used to provide certain "..........................".

A] References

B] Information

C] Points

D] Lists

Q.1. In formula bar, an adjacent range is specified by giving the starting and editing cell addresses separated by a

A] Semicolon

B] Comma

C] Full stop

D] Colon

INDUSTRIAL TRAINING INSTITUTE

Monthly Test-6, Marks- 20, Date:- _______________

(Every Question Carry Two Marks)

Q.3. A .... is a visual representation of data and conveys the information in an easy to understand and attractive manner.

A] chart

B] table

C] picture

D] graphic

Q.4. In formulas, a non-adjacent range is specified by giving the cell addresses separated by a ....

A] Semicolon

B] Comma

C] Full stop

D] Colon

Q.20. A "..............." is a prewritten formula the performs calculations automatically.

A] "Function"

B] "Equation"

C] "Template"

D] "Reaction"

Q.21. MS Excel 2007 is used for different types of .... varying from vary simple to complex.

A] calculations

B] manipulations

C] presentations

D] expressions

Q.25. While changing the level of an item in the hierarchy you can increase the indent by using.

A] "Tab"

B] "Backspace"

C] "Delete"

D] "Spacebar"

Q.27. To remove individual character at the left you may press "..............".

A] Delete

B] Backspace

C] Enter

D] Spacebar

Q.29. The intersection of a row and a column is called a "................".

A] Table

B] Cell

C] Data

D] Sheet

Q.30. A .... is a file that is provided by the application in a "ready to use" format.

A] Sheet

B] Template

C] Book

D] Report

Q.31. A .... is a visual representation of data and conveys the information in a easy to understand and attractive manner.

A] Chart

B] Table

C] Picture

D] Graphic

Q.35. "..........." are individual designs that can be applied to different parts to the document.

A] "Graphics"

B] "Styles"

C] "Pictures"

D] "Themes"

INDUSTRIAL TRAINING INSTITUTE

Monthly Test-7, Marks- 20, Date:- _______________

(Every Question Carry Two Marks)

Q.36. "..........." contains commands for opening, saving, printing, and closing a file.

A] "View" tab

B] "Office Button"

C] "Insert" tab

D] "Review" tab

Q.39. The text that appears in the top margin of the page is called the ....

A] Footer

B] Column

C] Header

D] Paragraph

Q.42. To stop the automatic relative cell references, i.e. to make the cell reference absolute, type a .... character before the column and row number.

A] # hash.
B] $ dollar.
C] % percent.
D] * star.

Q.5. "..............." refer to a ready-to-use picture.
A] "WordArt"
B] "ClipArt"
C] "SmartArt"
D] "Autoshape"

Q.8. The "............." tab contains tools that controls how to slide show is presented.
A] "Design"
B] "Slide Show"
C] "Review"
D] "View"

Q.10. .... which displays icon that represent commonly used commands such as Save, Undo, and Redo.
A] Home Button
B] The Ribbon
C] The Quick Access Tool bar
D] The Office Button

Q.11. A "..........." is a connection to a location in the current documnet, another document or a website.
A] Highlink
B] hipolink
C] linkage
D] hyperlink

Q.12. .... are used to create slide shows on the computer
A] Presentation graphics
B] Analytical development programs
C] Super Slide packages
D] Slide maker tools

Q.15. In graphic presentation, programmes each presentation is divided into ....
A] charts
B] slides
C] tables
D] pictures

Q.19. A "..............." is a pre-designed presentation designed for common purpose such as photo album or a quiz show.

A] "Chart"

B] "Table"

C] "Slide"

D] "Template"

INDUSTRIAL TRAINING INSTITUTE

Monthly Test-8, Marks- 20, Date:- ______________

(Every Question Carry Two Marks)

Q.43. A primary key must be

A] Unique But Permit Null.

B] Unique and Not Null.

C] Non-unique And Not Null.

D] Non-unique And Permit Null.

Q.44. which of the following are functions performed by a DBA?

A] Database Design.

B] System Security.

C] Backup and Recovery.

D] All of the above.

Q.45. "..........." is a relation database management application that is used to create and analyze a database.

A] Word 2007.

B] Access 2007.

C] System Security.

D] PowerPoint 2007.

Q.47. A "............" is a field or set of fields in your table that provide Access with a unique identifier for every record.

A] Password.

B] Special Code.

C] Primary Key.

D] Unique Code.

Q.51. what is the first step of defining a database.

A] Designing the database.

B] Collection of data.

C] Planning your database.

D] Digitizing your data.

Q.54. DBMS means..................

A] Database Management System.

B] Domain Management System.

C] Domain Manangeemt Server.

D] Domain Management Style.

Q.58 You can enter up to charactess in a text field.

A] 375

B] 125

C] 235

D] 255

Q.1. Netscape Navigator is a type of ....

A] Utility Program.

B] Operating System.

C] Browser.

D] Web Authoring Program.

Q.2. When you type an address such as "http://www.mkcl.org", in this .org indicates.

A] Original Web Site.

B] Commercial Web Site.

C] Organizational Web Site.

D] Educational Web Site.

Q.3. You can search the World Wide Web for a specific topic by using .... and.................

A] Gophers, Fido's.

B] Scanner, Search Engine.

C] Search Engines, Indexes.

D] Browsers, Larkers.

INDUSTRIAL TRAINING INSTITUTE

Monthly Test-9, Marks- 20, Date:- _______________

(Every Question Carry Two Marks)

Q.9. The network connecting several computers all over the world is?

A] Intranet.

B] Internet.

C] Arpanet.

D] Network.

Q.10. Which of the following is a browser.

A] Web site.

B] Microsoft.

C] Internet Explorer.

D] www.

Q.11. The terms DNS stands for.
A] Data Naming System.
B] Do Name System.
C] Domain Name System.
D] Duplicate Name System.
Q.12. Internet e-mail address is .... for every user.
A] Unique.
B] Same.
C] Common.
D] None of these.
Q.13. For navigating any website, user has to enter
A] URL.
B] www.
C] PPP.
D] None of these.
Q.14. What is the full form of E-Commerce ?
A] English Commerce.
B] Electronic Commerce.
C] Electric Commerce.
D] Element Commerce.
Q.15. To send e-mail to someone you need ....
A] Resident Address.
B] Internet Connectivity.
C] Fax Address.
D] None of these.
Q.16. .... is used to see the web page.
A] Inbox.
B] Recycle bin.
C] Internet Explorer.
D] Network Neighbourhood.
Q.17. Full form of URL
A] Universal Resource Locator.
B] Uniform Resource Locator.
C] Uni Resource Locator.
D] None of these.
Q.19. Which of the following is a search engine.
A] Google.
B] Alta Vista.

C] Yahoo.

D] All of these.

INDUSTRIAL TRAINING INSTITUTE

Monthly Test-10, Marks- 20, Date:- ______________

(Every Question Carry Two Marks)

2] <b> tag makes the enclosed text bold] What is other tag to make text bold?

a] <strong>

b] <dar>

c] <black>

d] <emp>

3] Tags and test that are not directly displayed on the page are written in _____ section]

a] <html>

b] <head>

c] <title>

d] <body>

4] Which tag inserts a line horizontally on your web page?

a] <hr>

b] <line>

c] <line direction="horizontal">

d] <tr>

5] What should be the first tag in any HTML document?

a] <head>

b] <title>

c] <html>

d] <document>

6] Which tag allows you to add a row in a table?

a] <td> and </td>

b] <cr> and </cr>

c] <th> and </th>

d] <tr> and </tr>

7] How can you make a bulleted list?

a] <list>

b] <nl>

c] <ul>

d] <ol>

8] How can you make a numbered list?

a] <dl>

b] <ol>

c] <list>

d] <ul>

9] How can you make an e-mail link?

a] <a href="xxx@yyy">

b] <mail href="xxx@yyy">

c] <mail>xxx@yyy</mail>

d] <a href="mailto:xxx@yyy">

10] What is the correct HTML for making a hyperlink?

a] <a href="http:// mcqsets]com">ICT Trends Quiz</a>

b] <a name="http://mcqsets]com">ICT Trends Quiz</a>

c] <http://mcqsets]com</a>

d] url="http://mcqsets]com">ICT Trends Quiz

11] Choose the correct HTML tag to make a text italic

a] <ii>

b] <italics>

c] <italic>

d] <i>

INDUSTRIAL TRAINING INSTITUTE

Monthly Test-11, Marks- 20, Date:- _______________

(Every Question Carry Two Marks)

1] Why so JavaScript and Java have similar name?

A] JavaScript is a stripped-down version of Java

B] JavaScript's syntax is loosely based on Java's

C] They both originated on the island of Java

D] None of the above

2] When a user views a page containing a JavaScript program, which machine actually executes the script?

A] The User's machine running a Web browser

B] The Web server

C] A central machine deep within Netscape's corporate offices

D] None of the above

3] _______ JavaScript is also called client-side JavaScript]

A] Microsoft

B] Navigator

C] LiveWire

D] Native

4] ___________ JavaScript is also called server-side JavaScript]

A] Microsoft

B] Navigator

C] LiveWire

D] Native

5] What are variables used for in JavaScript Programs?

A] Storing numbers, dates, or other values

B] Varying randomly

C] Causing high-school algebra flashbacks

D] None of the above

6] _____ JavaScript statements embedded in an HTML page can respond to user events such as mouse-clicks, form input, and page navigation]

A] Client-side

B] Server-side

C] Local

D] Native

7] What should appear at the very end of your JavaScript?

The <script LANGUAGE="JavaScript">tag

A] The </script>

B] The <script>

C] The END statement

D] None of the above

8] Which of the following can't be done with client-side JavaScript?

A] Validating a form

B] Sending a form's contents by email

C] Storing the form's contents to a database file on the server

D] None of the above

9] Which of the following are capabilities of functions in JavaScript?

A] Return a value

B] Accept parameters and Return a value

C] Accept parameters

D] None of the above

10] Which of the following is not a valid JavaScript variable name?

A] 2names

B] _first_and_last_names

C] FirstAndLast

D] None of the above

Monthly Test-12, Marks- 20, Date:- ______________

(Every Question Carry Two Marks)

Q. 1 ________ is the practice and precautions taken to protect valuable information from unauthorized access, recording, disclosure or destruction.

A] Network Security

B] Database Security

C] Information Security

D] Physical Security

Q. 2 ________ platforms are used for safety and protection of information in the cloud.

A] Cloud workload protection platforms

B] Cloud security protocols

C] AWS

D] One Drive

Q. 3 Compromising confidential information comes under__

A] Bug

B] Threat

C] Vulnerability

D] Attack

Q. 4 An attempt to harm, damage or cause threat to a system or network is broadly termed as _______

A] Cyber-crime

B] Cyber Attack

C] System hijacking

D] Digital crime

Q. 5 The CIA triad is often represented by which of the following?

A] Triangle

B] Diagonal

C] Ellipse

D] Circle

Q. 6 Related to information security, confidentiality is the opposite of which of the following?

A] Closure

B] Disclosure

C] Disaster

D] Disposal

Q. 8 ________ means the protection of data from modification by unknown users.

A] Confidentiality

B] Integrity

C] Authentication

D] Non-repudiation

Q. 9 _______ of information means, only authorized users are capable of accessing the information.

A] Confidentiality

B] Integrity

C] Non-repudiation

D] Availability

Q. 10 This helps in identifying the origin of information and authentic user. This referred to here as __________

A] Confidentiality

B] Integrity

C] Authenticity

D] Availability

Q. 11 Data ___________ is used to ensure confidentiality.

A] Encryption

B] Locking

C] Decryption

D] Backup

www.ingramcontent.com/pod-product-compliance
Ingram Content Group UK Ltd.
Pitfield, Milton Keynes, MK11 3LW, UK
UKHW021910190726
13853UKWH00002B/604